GARDENS
OF DELIGHT

INDIAN GARDENS THROUGH THE AGES

This edition published in the UK in 2008 by Pavilion Books
An imprint of Anova Books Company Ltd
10 Southcombe Street, London W14 0RA

ISBN: 978-18-6205-836-1

© Roli & Janssen BV 2008
First published in arrangement with
Roli & Janssen BV, The Netherlands
M-75 Greater Kailash II Market, New Delhi 110 048, India
Ph: ++91-11-29212782, 29210886; Fax: ++91-11-29217185
E-mail: info@rolibooks.com; Website: rolibooks.com

Editor: Priya Kapoor
Picture Editor: Ashita Murgai
Design: Supriya Saran
Production: Naresh Nigam

Printed and bound in Singapore

The vibrant colours of this eighteenth-century Mughal painting depict an
idealized marigold flower. Like all portrayals in Mughal miniatures, this
too, is characteristically two-dimensional.

Following pages: An aerial view of the strictly geometric Mughal Garden
at Rashtrapati Bhawan, New Delhi.

GARDENS OF DELIGHT

INDIAN GARDENS THROUGH THE AGES

RAHOUL B. SINGH

PAVILION

CONTENTS

Facing page: Shah Jahan's timeless monument dedicated to his wife Mumtaz Mahal in Agra, is set amidst a *char-bagh* garden, one characterized by its quadripartite composition and strong axiality.

Following pages: This unusual view of the stately Umaid Bhawan Palace in Jodhpur captures both the formality of the gardens and the enormous scale of the building. Designed by the Edwardian architect Henry Lanchester, the residence was originally called Chittar Palace, after the hill on which it is situated. The palace is set on twenty-six acres of land with fifteen acres of gardens.

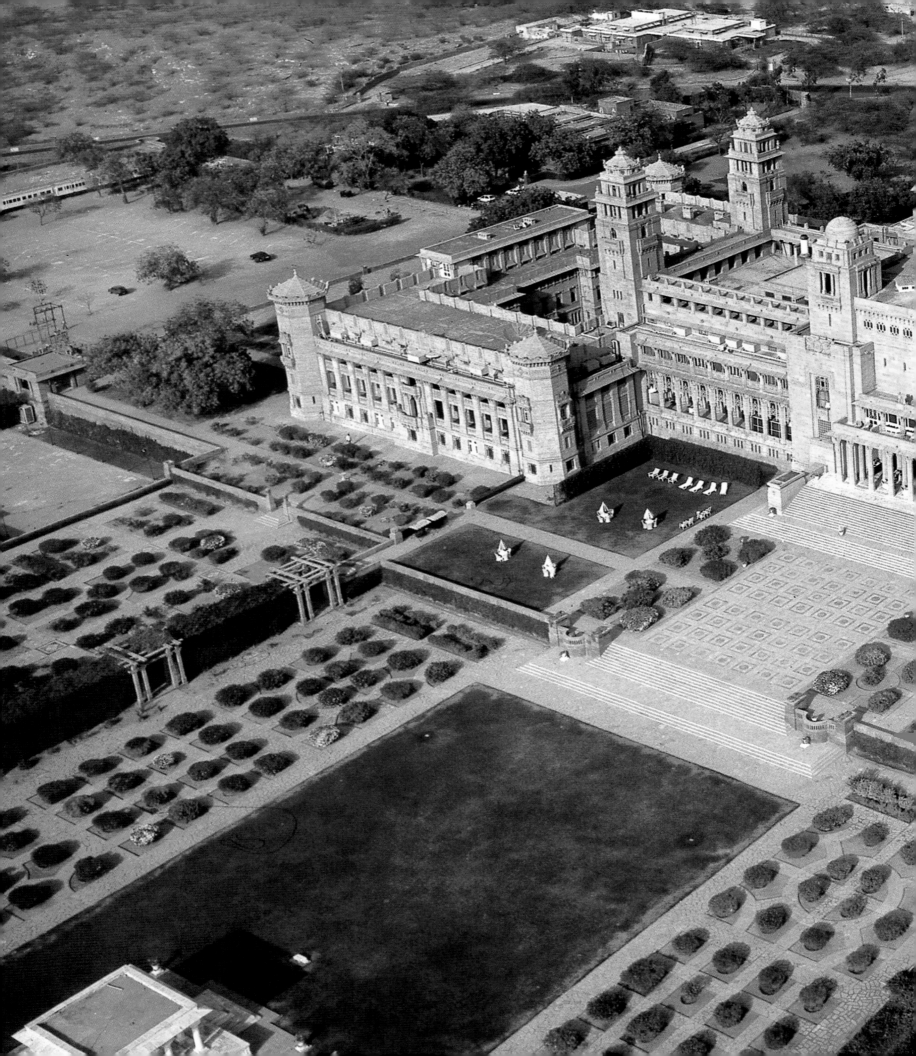

بدهل است کلانی او برابر سیب بوده باشد بویش بدنیست

غریب بیست و بمزه خیزنیست یک دیگر بیرست در فارسی

ACKNOWLEDGEMENTS

Both the writing and the production of a book is seldom, if ever, an isolated act. As with other books of similar nature, numerous people have contributed to *Gardens of Delight*, and one will always be greatly indebted to those who made it possible.

Whether it be to the writings of Ebba Koch, Catherine Asher, G.H.R. Tillotson, Partha Mitter, Deyan Sudjic, Christopher Tadgel, George Michell, D. Fairchild Ruggles, Glenn D. Lowry, Stephen White, Robert Irving, Kate Nesbitt, Robert Venturi, Pradip Krishen and Priyaleen Singh, who have all contributed substantially to the discipline and enriched one's understanding of it, or the numerous people who have slaved tirelessly and anonymously to write and post articles and listings on the internet, a great debt of gratitude is due. Their scholasticism has in ways direct and indirect greatly enriched *Gardens of Delight*.

The team at Roli Books have very patiently put up with the demands of a growing practice. Priya Kapoor has that uncanny ability to be both firm and polite, making it very difficult to say no to her (though I must admit I have been getting practised at it!), and her skills as an editor, publisher and project manager are enviable. Ashita Murgai and Supriya Saran have through their editorial prowess and graphic design sensibilities contributed immensely to the production of the book, as has Richa, who patiently and diligently went through the text, word for word. Without their contributions this book would not have been possible.

My extended network of family and friends, have over the last couple of months patiently endured the pressing demands on my time. Manifested in different, and at times surprising ways, their tolerance is greatly appreciated.

Lastly, this book, *Gardens of Delight*, is dedicated to that unsung hero of landscape and garden design, the gardener or *maali*, who toils selflessly in the summer sun to give us those delightful landscapes.

Facing page: An illustration from *Vaqi'at-i Baburi*, Babur's *Memoirs*, of a monkey jack tree.

11

INTRODUCTION

The Taj West End in Bengaluru was built in 1905 and is set in the midst of a twenty-acre property. As a product of India's colonial past the building and its gardens reflect the then prevalent attitudes towards landscape design.

While every invading force would like to leave an imprint on the land they conquer, there is no better way than through the taming of a landscape. A civilization as old and complex as India's is bound to have a highly evolved natural habitat, and while the intricacies of social order and hierarchy have undoubtedly led to the creation of environments of great variety, it is their gardens that form the cornerstone of this book. As with any form of artistic or cultural production, gardens too serve as historical markers. Their style and development tell of an attitude developed as much towards the natural environment as towards one's own worldview. Historically used as a political tool to ratify one's social position, or to establish an umbilical link with history, in as much as a means to cultivate herbal medicines or for the sheer sensory pleasures that one can derive from them, gardens have and continue to play a variety of roles.

This painting is from the *Razmnama* which is the Persian translation of the Sanskrit epic *Mahabharata*. Naqib Khan was commissioned by Akbar (ruled 1556-1605) to produce the translation for circulation to the Amirs in furtherance of Akbar's desire to promote understanding between Muslims and Hindus. Here Dronacharya is shown dying pierced with many arrows under an immense ficus tree, watched over by Krishna and the five Pandava brothers. The banyan symbolizes immortality and regeneration and placing the dying guru of the Pandavas under a banyan tree signifies his enduring legacy.

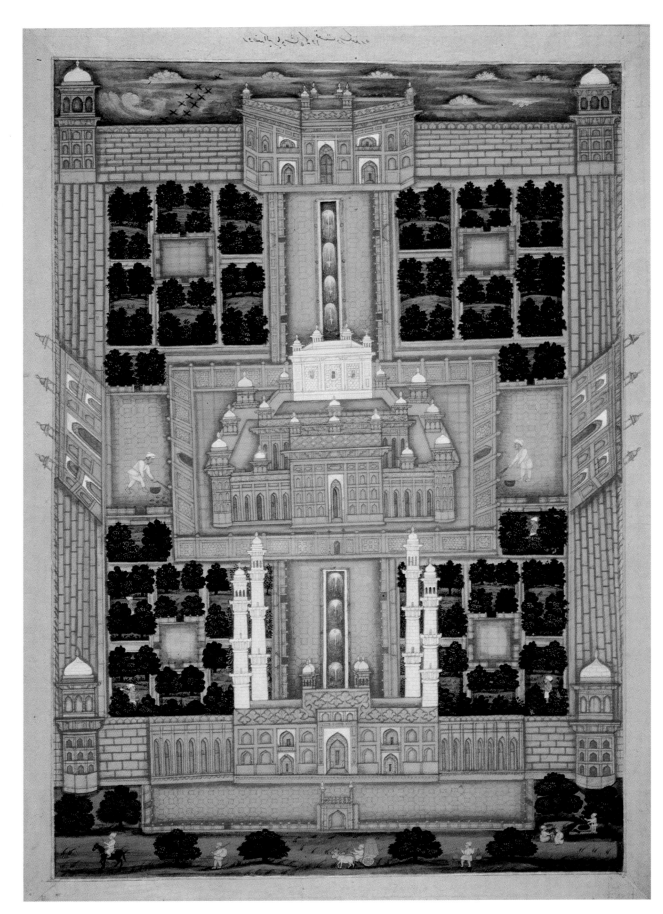

An unusual gouache painting of Akbar's Tomb at Sikandra, shown here both in plan and in elevation. Figures of sweepers, gardeners and passers-by can be seen on the road outside the mausoleum complex.

Whether through the compositional analysis of a particular garden or through the mythological and religious significance of trees and plants, this book attempts to present in part the long, varied and complex relationship shared between an ancient civilization and its garden history.

Unlike works of architecture that are housed inside them, a garden or landscape is rooted inextricably to the land within which it resides. Plants native to a region, the composition of the soil, climate and the availability of water, all play key roles in the construction of a garden. Dependent on the ever evolving seasons, the plantations in gardens are living constructs and hence need to be both cultivated and tended to. Furthermore, unlike say, a painting or a piece of sculpture, a garden is both always 'complete' yet never quite so. For instance, with years passing before trees reach a level of maturity, gardens are in a fairly literal sense, living works of art.

However large or small, gardens never existed in isolation. Dotted with structures that ranged from garden tents (*shamianas*) to palaces, these constructed landscapes enabled people to indulge in their primordial desire – to be one with nature. Pavilions, follies and viewing platforms further enabled one to enjoy picturesque views of the land, while through a process of selectively disallowing someone to access these structures established social hierarchy. Gardens have been and continue to be used as political vehicles in as much as they were created for the private pleasure of a select few. As spaces for congregation, parks such as Shivaji Park in Mumbai have been and continue to be used for political purposes.

Patronage has over the centuries taken on many forms. The great Mughal emperors articulated through their gardens an understanding of paradise. In modern India, while individual initiative led to the creation of the Rock Garden in Chandigarh, luxury hotel chains continue to commission landscapes that draw on historical precedent while working within a modernist idiom. In spite of the paucity of urban land, the desire for a home with a garden continues. Manifested as either terrace gardens or much larger and intricately designed palatial gardens, the residential garden continues an older and well established historical lineage.

The book is divided into four parts: Gardens Remembered; My Garden, My Paradise; Of Temples, Tombs and Palaces; and lastly, Modern India, Modern Landscapes. The descriptions of, and gardens presented do not represent an exhaustive list, nor are they intended to, but serve to illustrate the variety and complexity of a greater landscape tradition. Whether through treatise, pictorial depictions or literary accounts, the manner in which we record and remember our landscapes illustrates not only what we choose to remember but also, through a process of selection, what is important to us. The section titled 'Gardens Remembered' looks at just that. The number and type of gardens are numerous and while the section titled 'My Garden, My Paradise' describes a selection of them, it is in conjunction with the 'Sacred Trees' of India that one can begin to form an understanding of the deep-rooted inter-relationship between mythology, religion and nature in India. Whether they were a demonstration – an act of will as a means of communicating absolute power – or the desire to establish historical continuum, 'Of Temples, Tombs and Palaces' describes some of India's most potent gardens and landscapes and the sociological role they played. The last section, 'Modern India, Modern Landscapes' describes and addresses the role played by gardens that have been constructed over the last two hundred years – a period of transition for India, from a British colony to an independent nation. The gardens and landscapes constructed during this period tell of the great shift in the nature of patronage and the role gardens played in the framing of a national identity, one that was set against the partition of the Indian subcontinent.

While focusing predominantly on the gardens of India, the book does refer to a select few gardens located elsewhere in the world. Acknowledging that both cultural and artistic production do not occur in isolation, the intention was not to produce either a comparative analysis of gardens around the world or to use gardens as a metaphor for a social and political history of a land. However, it was felt that in order to garner a greater understanding of gardens and landscapes in general, it would be helpful to introduce a brief section on garden styles, some of which can be found in India while others influenced, in part, the development of a greater garden aesthetic. It is important to add here that some sites include subdivided spaces and other composite elements which are thus implicit in the reference to a single garden.

The images in the book have been selected with a view of not only illustrating the text but as importantly, to enable one to visually inhabit these gardens and their historical portrayal. Miniature paintings, photographs of carpets and gardens, literary references and drawings all contribute towards this end. While at times the choice of images was infinite, at others even basic documentation was hard to come by. In either case the overriding impetus was to portray the gardens in a manner that either supported a novel reading of them or served to supplement mere textual references with additional visual information.

Lastly, it is hoped that a book on gardens such as this, much like the gardens referred to, would serve to further our appreciation of the skilful manipulation of a landscape and the varied and multifarious impulses that led to their creation.

Built in 1588, the Dilaram Bagh and the adjoining Kesar Keyari's extensive geometric parterres have long been a tourist attraction. They offer expansive views of Amber Fort, Jaipur.

Following pages: This bird's eye view of a south Indian temple illustrates the prominent location that both temples and their adjoining 'sacred gardens' enjoyed.

Ragmala paintings such as this brought together literary, artistic and musical traditions. Here Malasri ragini is depicted as a beautiful woman preparing a bed in a garden, on which she scatters lotus petals that she has gathered in leaf baskets. The mood is of beauty created in anticipation of a perfect lovers' tryst. The green landscape is dotted with the lily, poppy and carnation, and the colourful bedspread echoes the vivid flowers.

GARDENS REMEMBERED

Symmetry, harmony, trees, flowers, shrubs and water in the form of lakes, ponds, pools, canals, channels or reservoirs, cascading as waterfalls or spraying water jets from fountains – all this and more make up the concept of a garden. Linked to architecture over the centuries in India, whether as temple gardens or the palace, tomb and pleasure gardens of the Mughals, gardens are an inextricable part of Indian history.

Oral histories and the act of remembrance have always played a critical role in the creation of a shared identity between a people and their land. While the collective consciousness of a culture along with the social construction of an experienced reality may be the result of a host of seemingly conflicting yet multifarious factors, it is undoubtedly the act of remembering that most potently equips and enables us to invent the future.

Sita finds Ram (seventh avatar of Vishnu) among the lotus blooms: at first he suspects her of infidelity, but the pair are reunited and live happily ever after.

Right: This miniature painting from the *Ramayana* illustrates not only the great epic, with Ravana marching towards the fortified walls but also the pavilion-like structure that is flanked on one side by a grove and on the other by formal gardens with fountains and water channels. The formal gardens are laid in a *char-bagh* formation.

Below: Lotus blooms, as depicted here in a painting, are manifested in the greater Indian landscape in many different ways. Whether in paintings, sculptures, fountains or even in buildings such as temples, the lotus has, as a result of its mythological potence, constantly served as a source of great inspiration for generations of artists.

पूजा जयपाइ
जावतादिनरहैं

द्वारिकाक्षोंप्रागिलाग
वतोम्राथौ

उधव

It would, however, be difficult, if not entirely unreasonable, to engage with the act of remembering as a tool to form an understanding of the relationship between a people and their land without first formulating an informed perspective on the medium which enables it and allows its further communication. The symbiotic relationship that is shared between the object of record and the manner in which it is recorded or communicated is thus paramount.

This relationship, in conjunction with the viewer, frames and places the work within the broader context of cultural production. When confronted with a civilization that has been endowed with a history as complex, encompassing and multifarious as India's or perhaps more accurately, that of the greater Indian subcontinent, one has to concede the existence of many histories of equal validity (a corollary to this would be that any history is but a partial history).

While the existence of multiple histories is nothing new, it is essential to acknowledge the critical role an author plays both in making a selection of what and how to depict an object, and the manner in which to do it. This, in conjunction with the historical and contemporary landscapes that dot the Indian subcontinent and the medium of their representation, forms the cornerstone of this book.

Irrespective of the devices used, which are varied and multifarious, artists and architects have to contend with the different facets of time and the different types of spaces (pictorial, aural and so on) available to them. For example, filmmakers construct a spatial sequence through a series of frames, a strategy that allows them to play with the space-time continuum. Cinematic time thus does not reflect perceived time in the real world, but does reflect it in our sensory experience of a film.

Above: Morning prayers at the Kalakshetra Foundation for Bharatanatyam dance held under a banyan tree. Banyan trees figure frequently in Hindu texts and subsequently in Hindu art. Their large, flat leaves have appeared on carvings in Besnagar and the Hill of Sanchi from around the second century BC and have also decorated the illustrations of Mughal literature throughout the centuries.

Facing page: A banyan tree spreads itself over Buddhist relics in the east Indian state of Orissa. The extensive shade provided by the tree made it a popular resting point for traders travelling by land.

Left: Lotus leaves and blooms spread themselves across a tranquil water body, floating towards the banks of Ajaigarh, a princely state founded in 1765 by Guman Singh, a Bundela Rajput.

Facing page: Frescoes from the Mulagandhakuti Vihara in Sarnath, where Lord Buddha spent the first monsoon.

While the medium of recording has changed drastically over the centuries, the earliest records of trees and gardens in India belong either to the oral tradition, or are manifested as engravings on columns, depictions on seals, or described in ancient texts such as the *Kalpavriksha* and the *Chaityavriksha*, which indicate that the worship of trees was an integral part of the greater Aryan tradition, many trees continuing to be revered as sacred in India.

Intricately linked to both religion and mythology, trees such as the Ashoka (*Saraca Asoca*) have long been considered sacred by Hindus, Buddhists and Jains alike. Lord Buddha, for example, is believed to have been born under an Ashoka tree in Lumbini whereas Lord Mahavira renounced the world under this tree. Kamadeva (the god of love) has the Ashoka tree dedicated to him. The tree even finds mention in the epic *Ramayana* as the 'Ashoka Vatika' (the garden of Ashoka trees) where Hanuman meets Sita to convey Lord Rama's message that he is on his way to rescue her. Widely considered to be the 'sorrowless tree' the Ashoka has over the centuries come to represent transformation to greater enlightenment and fulfilment.

Similarly, the banyan or the Indian Fig (*Ficus benghalensis*) and the peepal or Sacred Fig (*Ficus religiosa*) trees have long represented the Trimurti – according to the *Brahma Purana* and the *Padma Purana*, Lord Vishnu, the Preserver in the Hindu trinity of gods, hid himself in a peepal tree when the demons defeated the gods, which is why the tree is a symbol of Lord Vishnu. The peepal is the oldest depicted tree in India, its roots considered representative of Brahma, the trunk of Lord Vishnu and the leaves of Lord Shiva. First appearing on a seal in Mohenjodaro, a city a part of the Indus Valley Civilization, it is known in Sanskrit as 'Ashvattha', the tree of eternal life. It is also known as the Bodhi or the Tree of Enlightenment for it is under this tree that Buddha is said to have attained enlightenment.

The Great Banyan at the Botanic Garden in Kolkata is among the largest trees in the world and, along with other banyan trees, has long been revered as being symbolic of Shiva, the destroyer of ignorance and the embodiment of knowledge.

Of similar significance in Hindu mythology is the role of the lotus flower. Evocative of beauty, purity and divinity, the white lotus

ागीनतो विदरोपत्राःर्प्पा-घरसुधा।।श्रीकछराधिकाप्रतें के

ग्रोलिह्नं=आदासनीतांड़ीवलेहिध्सीऊ।।विलासकेरेहिता।।विरला

An illustration from the *Kamasutra*, the ancient Indian treatise on love, shows courting couples in a garden. Gardens have played and continue to play an integral role in the sociological milieu of the subcontinent.

is unique in that it flowers and fruits simultaneously. Symbolic of the goddess of wealth and prosperity, Lakshmi, Lord Vishnu's consort, it is often portrayed with the goddess seated on it.

The mention of plants and trees in ancient India is not limited to the realm of religion and mythology. *Sumansa*, the name given to flowers, translates quite literally to 'that which pleases the mind' – a term that reveals the aesthetic sensibilities of the people who lived thousands of years ago in the Indian civilization as well as the central role that nature and gardens played in their lives.

Innumerable texts and manifestos mention gardening and horticulture. Vatsayana's *Kamasutra*, for example, refers to the *Vrikshayurveda*, a text that provides guidelines for the construction and maintenance of gardens and parks, a skill recognized in ancient India as one of the sixty-four *kalas* (arts). The *Vrakshayurveda* begins, for example, with a passage that reads, 'He is indeed a monarch if his house has extensive gardens, spacious gardens containing large pools of water with lovely lotus blossoms over which humming bees fly . . . That may be regarded as the consummation of all happiness . . . (giving) intense pleasure to the mind.'[1]

Canonical Jain and Buddhist texts make similar references. For example, in describing the important components of a city, Jain literature refers to pleasure gardens (*arama*, *ujjana*) and tanks (*vapi*)

Above: The painting is part of an illustrated manuscript that depicts the *Brahmavaivarta Purana*, a medieval text. Animals, birds and insects are shown to inhabit forests filled with sacred fig trees such as banyan, peepal, jasmine, Ashoka and mango. The *Brahmavaivarta Purana* includes the *Brahmakanda* (Book of Creation) wherein Krishna, the incarnation of the Lord Vishnu, symbolizes the Supreme Brahman with Radha in the divine garden of Brindavan.

whereas the Buddhist text *Lalitavistara* offers a description of the pleasure gardens of the kings, Bimbisara and Ashoka. Likewise, the five hundred gardens laid out by Prince Siddhartha (later Buddha, the Enlightened One), around Kapilavastu also find mention in the text.[2]

This period was also witness to a very important sociological transition when royal gardens were made accessible to the public for the first time. For example, the Venuvana and Ambvana gardens in the vicinity of Kapilavastu, where Gautama Buddha spent his childhood, and the Jetavanian gardens near Sravasti, the capital city of the Kosala dynasty during Gautama Buddha's time, were initially royal gardens that were opened to the public. They were later made into retreats for monks of different orders, a prelude to the later development of monastic complexes with gardens integrated in them.[3]

Visiting the monastic university of Nalanda in AD 630, the Chinese pilgrim, Hsieun Tsang described the surrounding gardens in these words:

> . . . the temple arose into the mists and the shrine halls stood high above the clouds . . . streams of blue water wound through the parks; green lotus flowers sparkled among the blossoms of sandal (wood) trees and a mango grove spread outside the enclosure.

Accounts of travellers such as Hsieun Tsang are vivid descriptions of a people and their relationship with their land. Megasthenes, the Greek traveller who was sent as an ambassador to India by Seleucus I of Syria, visited the palace of Chandragupta Maurya and described it as follows:

> . . . in the Indian royal parks, tame peacocks are kept and pheasants which are domesticated, there are shady groves

The iconography in this exquisite painting is both telling and illustrative. Drawn from the Gulshan-i-Ishq (Rose Garden of Love) the depiction of peacocks, tigers, rabbits and deer, coupled with a stream and a water tank, along with both a structured view of the gardens and a relatively untamed landscape in the foreground contribute towards creating an understanding of the prevalent social structure wherein both the figures and the animals are orientated towards the centre of the composition.

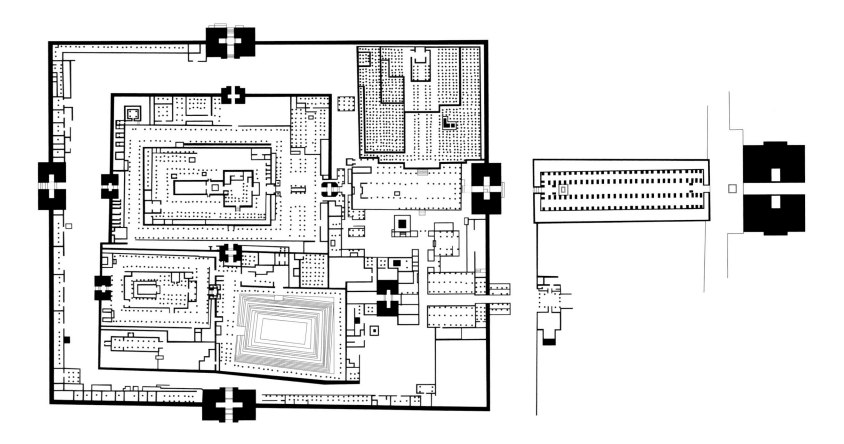

and pasture grounds planted with trees . . . while some trees are native to the soil, others are brought from other parts and with their beauty enhance the charm of the landscape.

This relationship of gardens with the perception of beauty, aptly summed up in the word *sumansa* (that which pleases the mind), is not without its accompanying prescriptive texts, which describe the modes and methods that one should follow when planning a garden. The *Kamasutra*, for example, states that every house should have a *vrakshavatika* or a *pushpavatika*, both terms referring to a garden that accommodates plants and fruit trees as well as herb and medicinal gardens.

Ponds, lakes, canals or tanks were other essential features to be found in these gardens. Apart from providing a relatively cool environment in the otherwise hot and sultry plains, these water bodies were also used for irrigation. A *variyantra* as described by Kalidasa, the Sanskrit dramatist and poet, was a novel device used to spray water on plantations – water flowed from fountains through narrow drains called *kulya* to irrigate the gardens, while water-wheels spurted jets of water into flowerbeds and circular ditches (*alavala*) at the base of trees. So elaborate were some of these systems that Kalidasa referred to one such palace garden and its

four accompanying fountains as Samudragraha,[4] which translates into 'House of the Sea'.

The sophistication that exemplified early landscape and garden design in ancient India was due in part to a number of treatises on the subject, the most famous and comprehensive of all being the *Vaastu Shastra*. Literally translated from the Sanskrit, the word *vaastu* refers to a site, building or house, while *shastra* refers to a treatise or instruction. Texts such as the *Manasara Silpa* (by Manasara), the *Mayamatam* (by Maya), the *Viswakarma Vaastu Shastra* (by Vishwakarma), the *Samarangana Sutradara* (by Raja Bhoja), the *Aparajita Priccha* (written by Bhuvanadevacharya, describing a dialogue between Viswakarma, the architect of the gods, and his son Aparajita), and the *Silparatna* comprise the vast *Vaastu Shastra*.

A critical component of the *Vaastu Shastra*, the *Vaastu Purusha Mandala*, describes both mathematically and diagrammatically the

Above: Plan and section of the Meenakshi Temple, Madurai.

Facing page: The lotus pond at the Madurai Temple complex with a sculptural golden lotus in the centre of the water tank.

basis for generating design. The *purusha mandala* is representative of a very specific *mandala* (diagram depicting the microcosm of the universe), which in the context of architecture and gardens, can be defined as a metaphysical plan of a building and site that reflects both the course of heavenly bodies and supernatural forces. Within the *mandala*, according to Hindu cosmology, the surface of the earth is represented as a square with gods and deities presiding over each direction (*ashtadikpalar*).

Among the greatest manifestations of the *purusha mandala* is the city plan of Jaipur, Rajasthan, in the form of a giant *mandala*, and the large temple complex in Madurai, Tamil Nadu, with its sacred pond where golden lilies once grew.[5]

The development of a treatise such as the *Vaastu Shastra* can only be a product of an evolved and structured society where art has dedicated patrons. As has been observed over the course of history, the nature of patronage in the arts has changed little. As was the case earlier, it continues to be the rich and the powerful who commission, build and subsequently use the built work (whether it be a garden, a painting or a building) to first project their worldview on to people and then to grow into it themselves (if they haven't done so already).

The medium chosen has always played as integral a role in communicating the message as the message itself. Sculpture, painting and architecture, for example, embodied varying degrees of transience, but were in themselves immobile, requiring people to come to them to view them. The oral tradition of the *mankha* or picture showman, who travelled with his painted scrolls and narrated the message to an audience, has historically been used as both a form of communicating a message as well as a means of entertainment.

Buddhism, as early as the first millennium BC, started commissioning works of art that were used to express its ideology. The emperor Ashoka (c.269-232 BC), for example, after succeeding his grandfather, Chandragupta Maurya (322-297 BC) was so shocked by the carnage in Kalinga (modern-day Orissa) after a war campaign that he adopted Buddhism as his religion and subsequently

Above: A gilded relief sculpture of Buddha's sermons showing him seated below a Bodhi tree.

Facing page: An aerial view of the Dhamekha Stupa, Sarnath, in the deer park, the site where Lord Buddha delivered his first sermon.

became a pacifist, espousing this view amidst his people and subjects.

In an astute political move, Ashoka enforced a code of behaviour that inculcated social responsibility in a vast and heterogenous empire where tensions between the clergy and the merchant class could potentially threaten stability.[6] Communicated through a series of inscriptions spread across his empire, this communicative strategy is most potently seen in the numerous Ashoka pillars that dot the Indian landscape.

At Sarnath, the site of the first sermon of Buddha, where he taught *dharma* (moral law) to monks, stands the great Ashoka pillar. Centuries later, adopted in part as a symbol of the Indian Republic, the sandstone pillar is characterized by four lions standing back to back and facing the four cardinal directions. Mounted on an abacus is a frieze of sculptures in relief work – the elephant, the horse, the bull and a lion, each serving to represent the different phases in Buddha's life.

The elephant symbolizes the conception of Prince Siddhartha (later known as Gautama Buddha), while the bull, according to the French scholar, Alfred Foucher, is indicative of the birth of Siddhartha during the month of Vaicakha (April-May). The horse depicts Kanthaka, the horse that Siddhartha rode while renouncing the material world for an ascetic life and the lion represents the attainment of Buddhahood.

While it may be argued that the pillars themselves announced the beginnings of monumental art in the region, one would have to sympathize with the historian John Irwin's argument that the emperor made effective political use of the numerous pillars spread throughout the empire by adopting a much older pillar/obelisk tradition, that is the *axis mundi*, as an agent to symbolize the centre of the known world (an ideology that is evident in numerous cultures spread across a wide historical spectrum).[7]

While the Ashoka pillar was constructed around the third century BC, a parallel oral tradition of communication was already fairly well developed. First in evidence during the sixth century BC, was the role of the *mankha*, a picture showman or travelling bard,

This painting from the 'Yuddha Kanda' of the *Ramayana* shows Hanuman in the Himalayas, the abode of gods, that are full of the holy retreats of ascetics, with peaks covered in plants and with streams rushing down to the river at their feet. The magical herbs, knowing that Hanuman has come to gather them, have made themselves invisible. But Hanuman, in his anger at being thwarted, simply breaks off the peak of the medicinal-herb mountain and flies back with it to the battlefield in Lanka.

as mentioned earlier, who continued to inform and entertain right up to modern India, his presence fading away only with the advent of television. A reference in the Pali canon, *Samyutta Nikaya*,[8] along with the knowledge that a strong tradition existed within Hinduism at the time, allows one to safely assume that Buddhist epics too were communicated in such a manner.[9]

Shortly after the death of Buddha, King Ajatashatru in 544 BC convened the first Buddhist council at the Sattapanni Cave in Rajgir (Nalanda district in the state of Bihar), to collate the teachings of Buddha. Known as the *Tipitaka* or 'Three Baskets', this canonical work was first communicated orally in Pali before being composed and translated into Sanskrit.

The king was both a follower of and a friend of Buddha. As narrated in the *Mulasarvastivadin Vinaya*, the monk Mahakasyapa commissioned Varshakara, a monk favoured by the king, to paint a scroll depicting the four great miracles of Buddha's life (birth, enlightenment, the first sermon, and death) as a means of informing the king of the death of Buddha (an image of a scroll with the four great miracles, 'Murals in a Maya Cave at Kizil', is on display at the Museum Fur Indische Kunst, Berlin). The scroll takes a portrait format and as the mural shows, is held up before the king just as a *mankha* would do.

It would be irresponsible to divorce the production of artistic culture from the greater social and cultural landscape within which it was set, and one cannot ignore an astute observation that Partha Mitter makes in his book on Indian art, especially while describing the manner in which Ashoka used art as a vehicle to keep in check an otherwise potentially explosive cocktail of religion and politics.

Describing early Buddhism, Mitter states that communal patronage vied with royal patronage and often 'royal or Kshatriya claims to divinity were held in check by the competing claims of the Brahmins', especially when 'kings used royal temples as a form of political legitimization when the temples themselves belonged to communities rather than to monarchs'.[10]

Left: The sixteen contemplations of the Sutra of the Meditation on the Buddha of Infinite Life.

This eighteenth-century miniature painting shows four women in an enclosed garden. A garden pavilion with carpets on the floor, and a parrot perched on a stand in the corner overlook, along with her attendants, a woman of the court.

This painting is a part of the *Javahir al-Musikat* (Jewels of Music), a Persian work on Indian music and the mystical feelings that are evoked by it. Sitting underneath a pomegranate tree, the long-limbed, slender woman is referred to as Bengali, which is a type of raga (a melodic mode of Indian classical music) but could just as convincingly be depicting a long-haired Bengali woman, who like the pomegranate, evokes feelings of generosity, sweetness, abundance and fertility.

The aspiration for immortality or at least the desire to ensure a legacy, along with the expression of will, is a trait that binds together some of the greatest patrons of the arts. And while the act of building is an agent for change, the process, often tumultuous and long, creates employment for masses of people while also demonstrating both the capability and resourcefulness of those commissioning it.

The decision to use the arts as a medium for the expression of will is not unfounded. The communicative potential of a work of art, be it a painting, a garden, a building or a work of music, stems as much from the directness of its approach, our sense perception and understanding of it, as the manner in which it engages and invokes both signs and symbols as tools to represent embedded ideals in the work.

The directness of approach while focusing itself narrowly on the expression of will and its associated intent is, as the architect Robert Venturi describes it, a technique of propaganda, its highly focused approach is also an instrument of reform. In being so, it is inevitably highly exclusive in the problems and issues it addresses and is, therefore, often the victim of over-simplification. A person engaged in such a project is 'at the risk of separating his architecture from the expression of life and the needs of society'.

Venturi elaborates by drawing our attention to the dichotomy presented by creations that have within them an embedded complexity and those that reside within the realm of the picturesque. Offering a critique of the modernist adage, 'Less is More', he observes that by bemoaning complexity and justifying its exclusion for expressive purposes, a work, irrespective of its medium, borders on the diagrammatic, a victim of its over-simplification. He astutely draws the distinction between 'the perception of what it seems and the conception of what it is', while simultaneously stating that the aesthetic simplicity which is so satisfying to the mind, derives from a far greater inner complexity.[11]

If Venturi speaks about the dangers of a reductive approach to a work, it would be worth pointing out that often within the narrowness of its intent, the propaganda used overtly employs symbols of a bygone era, sometimes juxtaposed with the specificity

of a local situation to establish both a historical link and purpose to the project at hand. However, in doing so, the opportunity to create a building, garden or art form that is culturally situated in the past, categorically acknowledges either an inability or a lack of vision in commissioning work that manifests the intent and desires of the society it is rooted in.

When viewing the arts as a communicative medium, it would be difficult to ignore that philosophical branch known as phenomenology. While it is well known that our understanding of the world is shaped by what we know, phenomenology addresses a more primordial question, that is, our being in the world as understood through sense-perception.

While, for example, the colour white represents joy in western cultures, but sorrow in the east (a bride wears a white gown in the west, while a mourner wears a white kurta pyjama at a cremation in India), so too are descriptions of distances dissimilar. Is the moon really 384,403 kilometres away or is it as it appears to be, hovering just behind the trees? Both descriptions are accurate and both equally relevant.

To communicate effectively, though one cannot rely solely on the use of any one device or strategy, mnemonic or memory devices can serve as very powerful tools, especially when invoking the uncanny or that which is vaguely and engagingly familiar. Alluding to either symbols of the past or signs that trigger memories, these devices, through a process of association, transform one's understanding of art from residing entirely and solely in the present

Above: A Mughal painting of Radha and Krishna seated in a grove, on the banks of a river with lotus blooms.

to encompassing a large cultural and historical continuum that is nevertheless rooted in the experience of the individual.

For example, the French Orientalist, Alfred Foucher observed that artists represented each stage of the life of Buddha through the use of specific symbols (the peepal tree representing his enlightenment, the wheel depicting his first sermon, etc.) that would become constant reminders of him.

Similarly, as extracts from *Sukhavativyuha Sutra* ('The Sutra on the Buddha of Eternal Life') as translated by F. Max Mueller show, in describing the 'Eternal Life' (paradise) not only does the *Sutra* make extensive use of such associative devices, constantly alluding, in this case, to nature and gardens, but also its vivid description and imagery engages with the reader's sense-perceptions.

And, O Ananda, the world called Sukhavati belonging to that Bhagavat Amitabha is prosperous, rich, good to live in, fertile, lovely, and filled with many gods and men. Then, O Ananda, in that world there are neither hells, nor the animals nor the realm of departed spirits, nor bodies of fighting spirits, nor untimely births. And there do not appear in this world such gems as are known in the world of Sukhavati.

Now, O Ananda, that world of Sukhavati is fragrant with several sweet-smelling scents, rich in manifold flowers and fruits, adorned with gem trees, and frequented by tribes of manifold sweet-voiced birds, which have been made by the Tathagata on purpose. And, O Ananda, those gem trees are of several colours, of many colours, and of many hundred thousand colours. There are gem trees there of golden-colour, and made of gold. There are those of silver-colour, and made of silver. There are those of beryl-colour, and made of beryl. There are those of crystal-colour, and made of crystal. There are those of coral-colour, and made of coral. There are those of red pearl-colour, and made of red pearls. There are those of diamond-colour, and made of diamonds.

There are some trees of two gems, that is, gold and silver. There are some of three gems, that is, gold, silver, and beryl. There are some of four gems, that is, gold, silver, beryl, and crystal. There are some of five gems, that is, gold, silver, beryl, crystal, and coral. There are some of six gems, that is, gold, silver, beryl, crystal, coral, and red pearls. There are some of seven gems, that is, gold, silver, beryl, crystal, coral, red pearls, and diamonds as the seventh.

Also noteworthy here is the detailed description of the plants, with both the number and type of stones used being mentioned. The opulence with which the 'Eternal Life' has been imagined, coupled with the imagery associated with gardens, is very telling. The description is almost typological in its content and the allusion to nature in describing the 'Eternal Life' introduces two themes that would have a direct influence in greater landscape and garden design.

However, in spite of the numerous references to both ambitious and elaborate building projects, and the presence of texts and treatises such as the *Arthashastra* and the *Vaastu Shastras*, very little in terms of ruins and relics actually survived until the arrival of the Muslim rulers from Central Asia. Part of the reason for this is the extensive use of building materials such as timber, thatch and plaster that did not withstand the severity of the Indian climate. Contrary to this, the building material for palaces, temples and other such religious monuments was stone, which, as a result, have survived.

Irrespective of the religion, kings in ancient India were tutored in theories of kingship by courtiers, poets, holy men and teachers who were not only familiar with the great epics such as the *Ramayana* and the *Mahabharata*, but also with treatises such as the *Arthashastra* and *Vaastu Shastras*. Embodied in these works was a belief that kings and nobles, through the power of religious ceremony, were superior to ordinary people. Infusing them with this sense of superiority and immortality was religion and by extension, its architecture, which explains the relative permanency of the building materials used in religious and royal architecture in contrast to domestic architecture.[12]

As an envoy visiting the Indian subcontinent, Megasthenes called on the court of the Mauryas during the fourth century BC at

their capital Pataliputra (modern-day Patna) and described it not only in much detail, but also made a comparison between the Achaemenid palaces of Persia and the series of gardens and open halls of the Mauryan capital.[13] The remains of Pataliputra along with a few remaining ruins in Kausambi and Sravasti, dating back to the sixth century BC, are all that survives of ancient India.

Of the surviving examples illustrating courtly life during the first and second century BC are relief carvings on the lintels (*toranas*) of doors depicting the *Jatakas* (folktales with animal and bird heroes) along with stories illustrating the life of Buddha at Bharut and Sanchi in central India. Similar depictions can be found at the caves of Ajanta and Ellora in western India. Dating from the late

fifth century AD, these murals attest not only to the keen powers of observation of the artists but also to their technical prowess. The murals show the gardens found outside the palaces to be enclosed by masonry walls, punctuated by gateways, containing fruit trees, ponds, birds, ducks, fish and other such features.

Above: Maharana Sangram Singh of Mewar (1690-1734), visiting the Ashram of Yogi Nilakanghgirli. The gardens of ashrams such as this have historically been used as places for meditation and preaching.

Following pages: An aerial view of the Lodhi Garden in New Delhi. The sixteenth century monuments are situated within the gardens designed by J.A. Stein and Garrett Eckbo in 1968.

VISION OF PARADISE
The Garden Carpet of Jaipur

Woven in Persia and brought to Jaipur in 1632 during the reign of Mirza Raja Jaisinghji, the Garden Carpet, which is twelve feet in width and twenty-eight feet in length, features the classic *char-bagh* iconography.

Interestingly, the four-fold composition that organizes Islamic gardens is used in the carpet as a device of pictorial composition. With water channels dividing the carpet into quadrants, smaller sub-divisions allow for greater flexibility, portraying both real and imagined landscapes.

While the great Garden Carpet with its intricate weave and multiple depictions probably took over a decade to make, the miniature Persian painting of 1686 titled 'A Vision of Paradise and the Deeds of Ali (cousin and son-in-law of Prophet Muhammed) and His Companions' portrays the Quranic concept of Paradise.

The painting, much like the carpet, depicts the *char-bagh* with water channels flowing into it but also shows a figure on the left (probably the Mughal Emperor Babur) instructing his workers on how to lay the garden, reading from a parchment. The octagonal waterbody in the painting is in sharp contrast to the square tank in the carpet. From the central viewing pavilion, with its motif-studded blue dome, the emperor could enjoy the grand vistas of the garden with its exotic animal and plant life.

With stylized representations of fish and ducks, lions and stags along with imaginary animals such as Keylin, the mythical Chinese unicorn, the carpet portrays the idea of Paradise both as a peaceful place and a hunting park characterized by violence and death, with predators swooping down on their prey.

The painting, apart from illustrating the laying out of a Paradise garden also shows a sage delivering a religious discourse to the uninitiated in the mid-ground. The reward promised to the faithful, the garden of Paradise is represented at the bottom of the composition.

The Muslim belief that Heaven and Paradise are represented by a garden, as mentioned in the Quran, is the primary motivating and inspirational force behind Islamic garden design. The following passages from the Quran describe the relationship between those who do good and gardens:

'For those who believe and do good, God has prepared gardens under which rivers flow, to dwell therein forever: that is the Supreme Felicity.' (9:100)

'For the righteous are gardens in nearness to their Lord, therein is their Eternal Home.' (3:15)

'And give glad tidings to those who believe and do righteous good deeds, that for them will be gardens under which rivers flow (in Paradise).' (2:25)

Facing page: This Persian miniature painting dated 1686, depicts a *char-bagh* garden in 'A Vision of Paradise and the Deeds of Ali (cousin and son-in-law of Prophet Muhammed) and His Companions'.

The Garden Carpet of Jaipur. Visible here are stylized representations of fish, ducks, lions and stags, along with Keylin, the mythical Chinese Unicorn. Aspects of both the Paradise garden and the hunting park are depicted in the carpet.

'For those who fear their Lord, are gardens under which rivers flow (in Paradise); therein are they to dwell (forever), an entertainment from Allah; and that which is with Allah is the Best for Al-Abrar (those who are obedient to Allah and follow strictly His Orders).' (3:198)

As a consequence of the Quranic texts and the descriptions of the gardens of Paradise, the message of Islam was spread far and wide. The depictions also served as a constant reminder of the deeds that were expected of a person, and the rewards (Paradise) that they would earn.

The idea of a garden representing a notion of Paradise and a description of rivers (water) finds mention in the Book of Genesis even prior to its Quranic references:

'(10) And a river went out of Eden to water the garden; and from thence it was parted, and became into four heads. (11) The name of the first is Pison: that is it which compasseth the whole land of Havilah, where there is gold. (12) And the gold of that land is good: there is bdellium and onyx stone. (13) And the name of the second river is Gihon: the same is it that compasseth the whole land of Ethopia. (14) And the name of the third river is Hiddekel: that is it which goeth toward the east of Assyria. And the fourth river is Euphrates.' (Genesis 2:10-14, KJV)

Interestingly, the passage tells us of the source of the water running through the garden before dividing into the four rivers.

The Garden of Eden, as described in the Book of Genesis, is where God placed Adam and Eve after He created them. Instructed to look after the Garden, Adam and Eve were forbidden to eat the fruit of the trees. Convinced by a serpent to disobey God and to eat the fruit from the Tree of the Knowledge of Good and Evil, Adam and Eve were subsequently punished by God for disobeying Him.

The passage describes water flowing through this garden before it is divided into the rivers to reach the plains and agricultural fields. The source of livelihood thus carried with it both the sins and the virtues of Adam and Eve.

The harnessing of the rivers, as depicted in the painting for cultivation or for the creation of the Paradise gardens, helps to perpetuate the belief in a king's divine powers, something that was further reiterated through the magical powers of royal ceremonies, and the microcosmic creation of and reconstruction of the universe.

Other ancient references to gardens in the Christian tradition confirm the umbilical link that the ancient religions, Buddhism, Hinduism, Christianity or Islam, had with an idealized view of nature and its portrayal as a promised land (Paradise) from where all life stems. For example, in the Song of Solomon iv.13: 'Thy plants are an orchard of pomegranates, with pleasant fruits; camphire, with spikenard; in Ecclesiastes 2.5: 'I made me gardens and orchards, and I planted trees in them of all king of fruits'; and in Nehemiah ii.8: 'And a letter unto Asaph the keeper of the king's orchard, that he may give me timber to make beams for the gates of the palace which appertained to the house, and for the wall of the city, and for the house that I shall enter into. And the king granted me, according to the good hand of my God upon me.'

Gauri ragini, wife of the raga Malkauns, is shown standing in the midst of a garden with marble pools. Banana trees frame the foreground while slender Ashoka trees can be seen behind her along with two garden pavilions.

MY GARDEN, MY PARADISE

Gardens, nature and notions of the picturesque have framed our worldview and have helped establish that intricate relationship between what we consider to be a worldly depiction of paradise and our primordial need to engage with the outdoors, whether as food-gatherers as in the past or in its more modern-day incarnation as those who harness the powers of nature for societal betterment. The manifestation of social impulsions such as spaces required for religious congregation, the building of memorials, the need and desire to hunt for either pleasure or sustenance or the creation of gardens, and their accompanying features such as pavilions, as a means of establishing social hierarchy, are all attributes of a developed society. In conjunction with their aesthetic appeal, such spaces have given us tremendous insights into the social and cultural milieu of the times they have belonged to.

Seventeenth-century painting of Mughal Emperor Humayun and his son and successor Akbar kneeling in a garden alongside lotus blooms.

While the recognition of the picturesque as an aesthetic ideal is a relatively new development, being introduced into the cultural debate as recently as 1782 by William Gilpin in England, it does include cultural notions of beauty and the sublime. Recognizing that beauty appeals to us sense-perceptively and is not necessarily a product of the rational mind but instinctual, the picturesque aligns itself with the romantic ideals of the eighteenth century.

Such notions were not isolated events and were firmly rooted within the greater historic continuum and used to invoke a sense of nostalgia that developed an individual notion of paradise.

Writing on typology in her anthology, *Theorizing a New Agenda for Architecture*, Kate Nesbitt argues that stripped of the manifestations of any form, 'type' too is a communicator of meaning. She adds, 'consciously or unconsciously perceived, type creates continuity with history, which gives intelligibility to buildings and cities (and gardens) within a culture.'[1]

The dual aspects of continuity and intelligibility that Kate Nesbitt refers to is equally valid within the realm of landscape architecture and more specifically, garden design. Some key typologies in garden design are described below:[2]

HOME GARDEN

The advent of the domestic garden can be traced back to the time of transition, when a society of hunters and food-gatherers changed gradually to a society that had settled permanently in one location. These gardens, generally enclosed by walls to ward off predators, were initially venues solely used to grow plants of medicinal value or to provide vegetables for domestic consumption. Subsequently, the leisured class began developing these gardens with a view to derive not only aesthetic pleasure from them but to also use them

Above: Dense and varied plantations engulf the residence of photographer Raghu Rai as a series of terraces and pavilion structures mediate between the garden and the house. The formality associated with a Mughal garden gives way to a landscape that enacts the practice of everyday living.

as spaces from which they could practise everyday living and entertaining.

In India, with the subsequent growing affluence of societies, it became fashionable for people to retreat to summer cottages at places of some altitude to ward off the harsh heat of the plains. Generally located in the foothills of the Himalayas, these cottages were first introduced to India by British colonizers. (The word 'cottage' in itself, however, derives from the thirteenth-century French word *cote* which refers to shelter. When adopted by the English language, the suffix 'age' was added and the term came to refer to the land that was with the *cote*.)

With flat lands in the plains available for cultivation and a more developed food-chain cycle, domestic gardens began to be used solely for leisure, with people often planting exotic trees and shrubs for sheer pleasure, along with those plants with religious connotations to them.

In urban centres where land was scarce and people often resided in apartments, the home garden re-invented itself into a terrace garden, often concrete, paved or with a complementary stone flooring, without any grass, but nonetheless exhibiting the same notions of delight and picturesqueness as some of their larger counterparts.

PARADISE GARDEN

The word 'paradise' in Persian describes 'a wall around' and originally referred to a hunting park. The word originated from *paradeisoi* (*pairi* meaning 'around' and *deaza* referring to 'wall').

Above: The lushness of the garden with statues, bells and a pool in the background belies a growing trend in residential landscape design that creates gardens for rejuvination amid the pressures of urban living.

Following pages: The Akshardham temple in Gandhinagar, Gujarat, is situated in the midst of a fifteen-acre garden, Sahajanand Van. The contemplative garden has within it pockets that are used for growing herbs. It also includes a children's park, a lake and a waterfall.

Fatehpur Sikri served as Mughal Emperor Akbar's capital between 1571 and 1585. The red sandstone city was abandoned due to lack of water. In contrast to the more formally structured Mughal city of Shahjahanabad (Delhi), Fatehpur Sikri is easily identifiable by its terraces and shifting axes.

The enclosures often contained exotic plants and animals acquired after military campaigns and co-existed with smaller enclosures for royal residences. The word 'paradise' came to mean 'heaven' when it was adopted by the ancient Greeks and became a symbol of heaven in the Abrahamic religions of Judaism, Christianity and Islam. Characteristic of these gardens is the combination of a walled enclosure with plants, birds, fruit trees and geometrical canals. A network of canals served both as a means of supplying water as well as an ornamental feature, the water reflecting the trees nearby. As retreats, secluded and insulated from the outside world, these gardens were often intended to be viewed from first-storey windows or from garden pavilions and were not conceived as spaces for outdoor living. A result of this was the often structured geometry of such gardens, which ultimately culminated in the development of the *char-bagh*, the four-fold garden.

As a quadripartite composition, with water canals segregating the sections, these Paradise gardens have Greek, Persian and Mughal antecedents. The Greeks explored the idea of the four elements (earth, water, fire and air) in their gardens while the Quran describes the Paradise garden as a garden of eternity (*jannat al-khuld*) with four rivers – of water, milk, wine and honey. The Mughals developed this notion even further with the numerous gardens that they built across their empires. Curiously, in spite of its nearly 2,500-year-old history, the geometry of the Paradise garden has changed little.

Preceding the strict geometry of the Paradise garden, the hunting park that it originated from took shape from the geometry

Above: Built by Prince Azam Shah, Emperor Aurangzeb's son, as a tribute to his mother Dilras Bano Begam during the late seventeenth century, the Bibi ka Maqbara ('Tomb of the Lady'), Aurangabad shares a resemblance with the Taj Mahal in Agra.

Facing page: The Pareshnath Jain Temple in Kolkata was built in 1867. Four temples constitute this complex, with the main temple honouring the tenth Jain avatar, Sri Sital Nath Ji. A stream flanked on both sides by flowerbeds and a garden with intricate paving patterns and statues belie European influences that had begun to influence ideas on architecture and landscape design.

and contours of the land. With large tracts of land coming into cultivation, kings began to look for places where plants could grow in the wild and animals could breed and proliferate in numbers so that they could be hunted. Often these large preserves would also be used as practice grounds for young men learning horse and chariot riding and the techniques of war.

The idea of a national park or of nature parks dates back to early Egyptian times when plants, trees and animals were believed to reflect the nature of the gods. In its modern incarnation, the national park or more aptly, nature reserve, is an area where people can observe and engage with 'untouched nature'.

Parks such as Kaziranga in Assam are home to two-thirds of the world's population of one-horned rhinoceroses and to the highest number of protected tigers in the world.

Mary Victoria Leiter, the wife of Lord Curzon (Viceroy of India,1899-1905), disappointed at not being able to see a rhinoceros, asked her husband to take appropriate measures to prevent the species' extinction. It was on 1 June 1905 that he began the creation of the Kaziranga Proposed Reserve Forest, which over the next three years extended to the banks of the Brahmaputra river. Covering an area of 430 square kilometres in 1908, it was designated a Reserve Forest and by 1916 was converted into a game sanctuary – the Kaziranga Game Sanctuary – and remained so till 1938 when hunting was prohibited. In 1950, it was renamed the Kaziranga Wildlife Sanctuary.[3]

TEMPLE GARDENS

As places of both congregation and sanctity, the spaces around a temple began to take on greater significance. Whether open to the

public or merely a place for the priest to preside over a religious ceremony within a protective wall, the temple garden became a sanctuary for meditation and contemplation. Buddhist temples, for example, often had gardens within the enclosures in deference to Lord Buddha who had meditated in one such park.

Often, entire groves were considered sacred, and were believed to be 'holy' or sanctified spots particularly suitable for ceremony. These sanctuaries often either had a statue of a god, a temple, a holy lake or religiously significant trees. The term 'a sacred grove' has come to refer to a landscape within which a sanctuary is located, the extended area of the sanctuary, or a group of trees within the sanctuary.

There are numerous references to sacred groves and temple gardens in ancient Sanskrit, Prakrit and Tamil literature. Kalidasa, for example, in *Mangalashtaka* writes of a grove of ten fruit-bearing

trees that he hopes will bring well-being into the world. Similarly, he writes about beautiful gardens where romance blossomed as princes and princesses played with their friends.

The forest of happiness that he writes about, also referred to as *nandavana* (fruit orchards), along with the *devavanas* or sacred groves (also known as *kaavu* in Malayalam, *devarakaadu* in Kannada, *kaadu* in Tamil or *oran* in Maharashtra and Rajasthan), formed the basis of the sacred groves found in south India.

While the *devavanas* were dedicated to the mother goddess, with ponds in which medicinal plants were grown, the *nandavanas* of the south could be further divided into five categories:

Tourists watch wildlife while riding on elephants through the Kaziranga National Park, the last home of *Rhinoceros unicornis*, the Indian one-horned rhino.

1. Exclusively floral gardens in which, among other flowers, jasmine, pandanus trees and shrubs and michelia bloomed. It was from these gardens that flowers were plucked to give as offerings to the temple and were therefore considered sacred. As the priest sometimes was also the village doctor, medicinal plants and herbs proliferated in these gardens as well. The temples of Veerasekhara at Thirukovilur and the Vedapuriswara temple grove are examples of this category.

2. The second category contained only fruit groves.

3. The third, such as the groves to be found at the Siva temple at Thiruvennainallur, contained both fruit trees and flowering plants.

4. The fourth category contained a single species of flowering plants, such as jasmine.

5. The fifth category, known to exist during the Pandayan and Vijaynagar periods, was an entire forest, maintained as a *nandavana*. The *nandavana* at Srirangam, for example, also known as the Madurakavi Nandavanam, sprawls across ten acres of temple land on the banks of the Kaveri river. The flowers from here are offered to the deity in morning prayers and also woven into garlands.[4]

Historically documented in sacred texts, literature and epigraphs, gardens played a pivotal role in the religious lives of people, with festivals arranged to celebrate their sanctity and to conserve them as well.

There are three main temple festivals that celebrate the sacred groves. The spring festival or *vana mahotsava*, which is celebrated on the full moon day within the holy grove. The deity, the mother goddess, is worshipped through the night after a procession through the grove (*nandavana*).

The second festival, known as the sacred hunt or *thiruvettai*, was referred to in an inscription of the Chola king, Rajaraja II. A bronze *utsava murthi* of Shiva depicted as a hunter was taken to

Above: The Sun Temple at Konarak is a colossal chariot of the sun god (Surya) drawn on twelve pairs of wheels by a team of seven horses. Twelve wheels, possibly symbolizing the twelve months, are carved into the terrace and on each side at the front.

Facing page: The Tirukkalikundram Temple complex in Tamil Nadu, set against a lush green landscape, can be seen here with its key design elements and two adjoining water tanks.

A HINDOO PLACE OF WORSHIP.

Above: An early illustration of a Hindu place of worship, Thomas Daniell, William Orme, Joseph Constantine Stadler, circa 1804.

Left: A historic view of Srirangam. The traditional temple structure (as seen in the background) contrasts sharply with the contemporaneous domestic architecture of the time (as visible in the foreground).

the sacred grove where he was enthroned for several days in homage to the sanctified plants growing in the grove.

A third festival similar to *thiruvettai* called *vasantha thoppu* was also conducted in the spring.[5]

BOTANIC AND ZOOLOGICAL GARDENS

Early Chinese emperors, Egyptian pharaohs and Babylonian kings, all kept plants within walled enclosures, marking the beginning of botanic gardens. Initially, these gardens were no more than a collection of plants. The modern botanical garden, like modern science, is a construct of the Renaissance, with the Orto Botanico in Padua, Italy, being one of the oldest examples. Initially laid out on the estates of either royalty or rich noblemen, botanic gardens were at times combined with zoological gardens in which exotic beasts were kept. In their modern-day incarnation, zoological gardens are now also centres for research and education.

The Indian Botanic Garden in Howrah (Kolkata) is both the largest and oldest of such gardens in South Asia. Established in 1787 by Lieutenant Colonel Robert Kyd, a British army officer stationed in India, the gardens are spread over 273 acres along the west bank of the Hooghly river. The landscaping, designed initially by Sir George King in 1782, comprises artificial lakes, undulating land, an underground network of irrigation pipes and interconnected moats. With over 12,000 trees and shrubs belonging to 1,400 different species, the gardens were first known as East India Company's Garden or Company Bagan, and later as the Royal Botanic Garden.

Millions of visitors come to the gardens to see the Great Banyan (*Ficus benghalensis L.*), a gigantic tree with 2,800 prop roots that have over the last 250 years proliferated to cover 1.5 hectares. Among the numerous plants to be found in the gardens, greenhouses and conservatories are over a hundred varieties of palms, a plethora of aromatic plants and a medicinal-plant garden known as the Charak Udyan.[6]

The banyan tree with its complex network of aerial roots is representative of the gods Vishnu, Shiva and Brahma, and is symbolic of life and fertility. This banyan tree (right) is located in Ranthambore.

Designed by Lieutenant Colonel Sir Michael Filose and commissioned by Jayaji Rao Scindia (1843-86), the Jai Vilas Palace in Gwalior incorporates a number of architectural styles such as Doric, Tuscan, Corinthian, and Palladian. It is among the larger palaces in India.

SACRED TREES

HINDOO TEMPLES AT AGOUREE, ON THE RIVER SOANE, BAHAR.

Aqua tint with watercolour on paper: Hindu temples on the banks of the river Soane with travellers resting under a banyan tree in the foreground.

Indian mythology and the symbolism associated with trees share an intricate relationship in history. As numerous references in ancient texts and epics show, trees in India are representative of gods, goddesses and their relationships. This is due in part to the medicinal, particularly ayurvedic and herbal, properties that are to be found in the flowers, leaves, barks and roots of trees.

The species of the trees in themselves are very old, originating from Vedic times and often have multiple meanings and references. They are worshipped and revered in different ways too but have a rich history apart from the more conventional accounts of their origin.

The trees mentioned below do not present an exhaustive list but describe briefly some important trees, their mythological significance and the roles they play in Indian society.

ASHOKA

The Sanskrit word *ashoka* translates broadly into 'without grief' or 'that which gives no grief'. The tree is considered sacred by the Hindus and is dedicated to Kamadeva, the god of love. The tree also finds mention in the *Ramayana* as the grove of Ashoka trees, Ashoka Vatika, where Hanuman first met Sita. According to Buddhist legend, Buddha was born under this tree in Lumbini, while the Jains believe that Lord Mahavira renounced the world under an Ashoka tree in Vaishali.

The tree belongs to the legume family and the *Saraca* genus. It is small, evergreen, and bears fragrant orange flowers that later turn red.

The belief is that drinking the water in which petals of the Ashoka flower have been washed takes away grief, the soothing qualities of the concoction working very gently as it changes a person's perception of sorrow.

BANYAN

The banyan tree, much like the peepal, is representative of the three gods, Vishnu, Shiva and Brahma. Symbolic of life and fertility, this tree is seldom cut and can grow to a considerable size, the Great Banyan in the Indian Botanic Garden in Howrah being among the largest trees in the world.

The national tree of India, the tree was originally called *F. benghalensis*, but early travellers visiting the subcontinent noticed that the tree was frequented by Indian traders or *banias* who rested and transacted business in the shade of its spreading canopy. It is for this reason that the Portuguese, followed by the English in 1634, began to refer to the tree as the 'banyan' or the tree under which Hindu merchants carried out their trade. In Gujarati, the word 'banyan' refers to a trader and not to a tree.

An 1829 engraving of a banyan tree

John Fleming, who served in the Indian Medical Service from 1768 to 1813 in Bengal was temporarily in charge of the Royal Botanic Garden. A part of his collection of botanical subjects included a series of watercolour paintings of plants such as this one.

Centre: A print that was first published in H.A. Van Rheede tot Draakenstein's *Hortus Malabaricus* was the result of a regional botanical survey undertaken in the Malabar Hills of the Western Ghats.

LOTUS

The lotus, the national flower of India, is sacred to Buddhists and Hindus alike. In Hindu mythology, it represents God, rising up in all His beauty from the murkiness around. Lotus plants grow both in swamps and in water, and can, depending on the depth of the water, grow up to six metres in height and as much as three metres in width, with leaves as large as sixty centimetres (flowers have been known to grow to twenty centimetres in diameter); they are unique in that they bear fruit and flowers simultaneously. Representative of Lakshmi, the Hindu goddess of fortune and prosperity, the lotus flower symbolizes spiritual enlightenment, divinity, fertility, wealth and knowledge. Hindu deities are often depicted seated on lotus leaves and meditating yogis traditionally sit in *padmasana* or the lotus posture.

According to Buddhist legend, Siddhartha Gautama was born with the ability to walk and wherever he stepped, a lotus flower bloomed. Another legend has it that after attaining enlightenment, Buddha was reluctant to teach *dharma* and was persuaded only after he saw a lotus stem extending from the bottom of a pond high into the air to embrace sunshine. This sight drew his attention to that small group of people who were not caught up in material pursuits or sensuous pleasures and were, like the lotus stem, willing to extend themselves to reach deep truth.

In Southeast Asia the plant has innumerable uses. Its seeds, leaves, flowers and rhizomes are edible and form the ingredients of soups and stir-fried dishes. The seeds, when boiled and made into a paste, are combined with sugar to make pastries such as mooncakes and rice-flour pudding.

NEEM

The neem tree not only has numerous medicinal benefits but is greatly revered by Hindus as a manifestation of the Goddess Durga or Maa Kali.

Historically, on the first day of Chaitra, after *amavasya*, people worship the neem tree and eat its leaves. Mixed with sugar and pepper, it prevents fever. Scientifically named *Azidirachta indica*, the tall evergreen tree sheltered Surya (the sun god) from the demons according to the *Brahma Purana* and the *Padma Purana*. It is rich in medicinal properties and, even today, people chew on neem twigs instead of using a toothbrush. Its fibres cleanse the teeth and gums and the juices act both as a dentifrice and a mouth-freshener.

In Tamil Nadu, while worshipping Maa Kali, women dress in red, and brandish the branches of the neem while dancing, as an act of purifying the world. In West Bengal, the neem tree is believed to house 'Sitala', the cure of all diseases, specifically of chicken pox, which is treated by rubbing the leaves on the body while praying to Sitala.

A drawing of a neem tree with its small round berries. Revered for its medicinal value, the neem continues to be a staple ingredient in many ayurvedic medicines.

The Peepal or Bodhi Tree, is sacred to both Hindus and Buddhists. The adjoining painting by the Victorian artist Marianne North (1830-1890) was showcased in the North Gallery in Kew Gardens in 1881.

PEEPAL

Worshipped ever since the Indus Valley Civilization (3000-1700 BC and first depicted on a seal discovered in Mohenjodaro, the peepal tree (*Ficus religiosa*) is also known as Ashvattha in Sanskrit. It was used during the Vedic period to start fires through friction and continues to be used extensively in ayurvedic medicine.

Symbolically, the peepal represents Lord Vishnu and it is believed that not only was he born under this tree but when the demons defeated the gods he found refuge in it. Lord Krishna too is associated with the peepal and in the *Bhagavada Gita*, he says, 'Among trees, I am the ashvattha.' It is believed that he died under this tree as well.

Known to the Buddhists as the 'Bodhi Tree' or Tree of Enlightenment, it is the tree under which, after forty-nine days of meditation, Shakyamuni Buddha attained enlightenment. The tree that now stands in Bodh Gaya in modern-day Bihar is a direct descendant of the sacred Bodhi. In the third century BC, Emperor Ashoka's daughter Sanghamitta, a Buddhist nun, carried a shoot of the tree to Sri Lanka. It was planted by King Devanampiyatissa at the Mahavira monastery in Anuradhapura and continues till today to be the oldest documented tree.

Hsieun T'sang, the Chinese traveller visiting India, had said: '. . . the tree stands inside a fort-like structure surrounded on the south, west and north by a brick wall. It has pointed leaves of a bright green colour . . . there is a large trench in the shape of a basin and devotees worship it with curd, milk and perfumes such as sandalwood and camphor.'

Centuries later, the British archeologist Alexander Cunningham noted, 'In 1862 I found this tree very much decayed; one large stem to the westward with three branches was still green, but the other branches were barkless and rotten. I next saw the tree in 1871 and again in 1875, when it had become completely decayed, and shortly afterwards in 1876, the only remaining portion of the tree fell over the west wall during a storm, and the old Peepal tree was gone. Many seeds, however, had been collected and the young scions of the parent tree were already in existence to take its place.'

SANDALWOOD

Also known as Chandana in Sanskrit, its scientific name being *Santalum album*, the evergreen sandalwood tree is native to south India, parts of Indonesia and Australia.

Vedic texts record that the scent of this tree is believed to have filled the Gardens of Paradise. Considered the epitome of excellence (in Sanskrit, that which is excellent is referred to as *chandana*), it is used extensively both in sacred ceremonies and to purify temples.

Sandalwood oil and paste have a cooling and calming effect on the body. In fact, legend has it that Lord Ganesha was created by the Goddess Parvati out of a sandalwood paste that she used for her bath and then breathed life into it. Often seen smeared on the foreheads of devotees of Vishnu and Shiva, its paste is meant to cool and protect the 'Agna Chakra', the nerve centre between the eyebrows. Generally depicted with serpents entwining it, the tree is also symbolic of inner strength and has historically been used to heal the skin from infectious sores, ulcers, acne and rashes.

In 1792, the Sultan of Mysore declared sandalwood to be the royal tree and in modern India every such tree is under the protection and ownership of the government in an attempt to prevent illegal smuggling of its fragrant wood.

This illustration of sandalwood is part of the Fleming Collection. The tree was declared to be a royal tree in 1792 by the Sultan of Mysore. Its fragrant wood is much sought after.

SANTALUM ALBUM

A natural antiseptic, the tulsi or sacred basil has long been used to cure a number of ailments.

TULSI

Sacred among the Hindus, the tulsi (sacred basil) is revered as much for its medicinal value as for its spiritual qualities. This shrub is unique in that, unlike other plants, it emits oxygen at night. A sociological implication of such an anomaly was that the tree was planted in courtyards where families would sleep to escape the summer heat. It is believed that the tulsi ensures the presence of Brahma, Shiva and Vishnu wherever it grows.

According to the *Devi Bhagavata Purana*, two of Lord Vishnu's three wives, Lakshmi and Sarasvati once quarrelled with each other. Sarasvati cursed Lakshmi, forcing her to live on earth forever as a tulsi plant. Blessed by a boon from Brahma, the demon Shankhachuda, Tulsi's husband, could only be defeated in war if his wife was unfaithful to him. Arrogant in the belief that he was invincible, Shankhachuda's behaviour made him very unpopular among his subjects.

Lord Vishnu sent Shiva to kill the demon while he assumed the form of Shankhachuda and seduced tulsi. Enraged when she discovered Vishnu's deception, tulsi was about to curse Lord Vishnu when he explained that she was indeed Lakshmi and he Lord Vishnu. Upon returning to heaven, it is believed that Lakshmi's hair became the tulsi plant while her body was transformed into the Gandaki river.[1]

To celebrate this event every year during the month of Kartik, the Vaishnavas marry a tulsi plant to a Shalgrama stone in modern-day Vadodara.

BAEL TREE

This deciduous tree has thorny branches and trifoliate leaves, their shape signifying Lord Shiva's three eyes and hence was seldom used as firewood except in the case of sacrificial fires. It has for centuries been offered to Lord Shiva in the belief that the cooling effect of the leaves will appease the hot-tempered deity.

According to the *Skanda Purana*, the bael tree grew from Parvati's perspiration which fell to the ground while she was performing penance. It is also known to be an emblem of fertility. The history of this tree, which grows wild all over the sub-Himalayan forest, can be traced back to the Vedic period, to around 2000 BC. A mention of it even appears in the *Yajur Veda*. The Jains consider the bael tree sacred too. It is said that the twenty-third Tirthankara, Bhagwan Parasnathji, attained nirvana, or enlightenment, under the bael tree.

Among its numerous medicinal values, the bael tree is anti-parasitic, anti-pyretic, a digestive and a laxative. It is believed that the fruit also nourishes the heart and the brain, which is why it forms the basis of many ayurvedic and *siddha* formulations.[2]

IMLI

A large deciduous tree native of Africa, it was brought to India so long ago that it is virtually considered to be indigenous and can be found in the warm, frost-free regions of the Indian subcontinent. Its flowers are pale yellow, often having orange or red streaks, while the fruit is a brown pod-like legume, which contains a soft acidic pulp and many hard-coated seeds. With a high vitamin C, tartaric, citric and malic acid content, the fruit pulp is used to treat a number of ailments that vary from fevers, digestive disorders and even poisoning. Used to prepare Rasam, Sambhar and an assortment of chutneys, in both north and south India, its tart fruit has become a staple ingredient in the cuisine of India.

India's oldest botanical gardens are in Kolkata, where the Scottish botanist, William Roxburgh (1751-1815) spent many years studying the country's flora while working for the East India Company. Of the tamarind tree he wrote, 'The tree is one of the largest in India, with a most extensive large, shady head, the bark dark-coloured and scabrous, the wood hard, very durable and most beautifully veined.'

An early twentieth-century lithograph of a eucalyptus from the 'Encyclopedie de la Plante'.

EUCALYPTUS

The tall evergreen eucalyptus with its petalless flowers can be found throughout the country. Its flowers and their buds, generally found in clusters of five to eleven are easily identifiable by their long, conical 'pixie caps'. The caps drop off to reveal a series of densely packed white stamens. While the leaves are sickle shaped, long and narrow, its fruit is manifested as a series of woody capsules with four to five 'teeth' that open to release the seeds once they are ready.

Used extensively to make paper in India, the eucalyptus is a fairly versatile and adaptable tree and can be found in both dry tropical climates as well as in moist forests. It was planted extensively in India during the 1960s as a tree intended to be used for agro-forestry.

KAIM

The kaim or kadamb tree was considered holy and can be seen in depictions of Lord Krishna in Brindavan; also in Buddhism, the tree was thought to reunite separated lovers. The tree is quick to grow and spread with glossy green leaves and produces a golden ball of flowers. The bark is grey and its fruit is characterized by a tight cluster of 100 to 150 'round heads' or globules. While the bark and root of this tree have traditionally been used to treat ailments such as colic and fever, its leaves are nutritious fodder. Kadamba flowers are an important raw material in the production of *attar* (fragrant essential oil of flower/plant), along with sandalwood.

The kadamb tree, umbrella-like, casting itself over Lord Krishna and Radha.

An aerial view of Agra Fort showing the historic encampment enclosed within its walled gardens.

An eigteenth-century watercolour-on-paper painting of a Martagon lily.

Facing page: A bird's eye view of Jag Mandir in Udaipur. Located in the midst of Lake Pichola, the palace was constructed by Maharana Karan Singh to serve as a refuge for Prince Khurram (later known as Emperor Shah Jahan).

OF TEMPLES PALACES AND TOMBS

A dominant landscape aesthetic and more specifically, a garden aesthetic, was brought to India with the advent of Islam. Taking advantage of the political turmoil and dynastic rivalry in northern India, Mahmud of Ghazni invaded India repeatedly during the first three decades of the eleventh century but never established a permanent presence in India, preferring to return to his home in what is now modern-day Afghanistan.

By 1185, another Turkish adventurer from Afghanistan, Muhammad Ghuri, had invaded the subcontinent and had reigned over Lahore. The Sultanate of Delhi was established in the 1190s when Ghuri was assassinated and his former slave, Qutub-ud-din Aibak succeeded him, founding the Slave Dynasty. His son-in-law Iltutmish (1211-36), a man of letters, was the next sultan and completed the famous minaret, the Qutub Minar (begun by Qutub-ud-din Aibak).

This opaque watercolour, painted in 1590, titled 'Babur Supervising the Laying Out of the Garden of Fidelity', illustrates key elements that would come to define later Mughal gardens: the *char-bagh* or quadripartite garden, water canals and the wall enclosing it. Also evident are the exotic trees and plants.

A turbulent political climate, coupled with a Mongol invasion and the subsequent capture of northern Punjab in the 1230s, left the greater part of northern India in a state of chaos before Ghiyas-ud-din Balban, a Turkish noble, seized the throne in 1265. After his death in 1286, the Afghan Khiljis won the throne and for the first time admitted both fellow Afghans and Indian Muslims into positions of authority in the government.

Ala-ud-din Khilji (1296-1316), in a span of twenty years consolidated his position and took the sultanate to its zenith. He withstood the onslaught of the Mongols till 1306 when they were forced to retreat, and the Rajputs lost two of their strongholds, Chittor and Ranthambore, to him. In the east, the Solankis of Gujarat and the Paramaras of Malwa, lost territory to the sultanate. In the Deccan he overcame the powerful fortress of Devagiri, the stronghold of the Yadavas, after which he reduced a number of smaller states to subjection.

Unfortunately, his successors, Ghiyas-ud-din Tughlaq (who began his reign in 1320) and then his son Muhammad could never quite match the might of the early Khilji reign. A diminished treasury and the subsequent greater taxation of agricultural produce, in conjunction with the attempt by Muhammad Tughlaq to re-locate the capital from Delhi to Devagiri, further depleted the already scant resources and ended all Tughlaq aspirations of empire building.

Two Hindu brothers who had been captured and forced to convert to Islam during the reign of Ala-ud-din Khilji had, in 1336, established a stronghold that would later develop into a kingdom at

Above: A watercolour and gouache-on-paper painting of a Mughal princess being entertained by female attendants in her palace garden.

Following pages: The Lake Palace with a pool and fountain occupying a central place in the courtyard with the adjoining plant motif paving.

ولادت همایون شد امراو غیر امرا خورد و کلان سلیخوا آوردند

Sur Gujarati's painting, depicting the celebrations in honour of Humayun's birth, illustrates the central role gardens, and specifically the *char-bagh* played in the sociological milieu of the time. The brightly coloured tent-like garden pavilion was a structure intimately familiar to Babur.

Hastinavati (Hampi). The two brothers, Harihara I and Bukka I, built a new capital in the Deccan known as Vijayanagar. With their tight control of the lucrative spice trade and the power of local temple authorities, the largest landowners in the Deccan, this period saw both the expansion of the last great Hindu empire and a proliferation of temples throughout the region. Excavations show the remains of a well-connected water distribution system within the royal enclosure and the large temple complexes with sophisticated channels used to supply water.

The Vijayanagar empire under the leadership of Krishna Deva Raya (1509-30) defeated the Hoysalas after a long and bloody battle. In an astute move, Krishna Deva allowed the defeated Bahmani rulers to remain in Bidar. Unfortunately, eight years after his death, factional rivalry caused the ouster of the Bahmanis with the successor states of Ahmadnagar, Bidar, Berar, Bijapur, Khandesh

and Golconda rising up against the Vijayanagar state and defeating them in 1565.[1]

Almost concurrently, in the north, Zahir al-Din Muhammad Babur, the first of the Great Mughals, defeated Ibrahim Lodhi of the Delhi sultanate in the battle of Panipat in 1526. Babur died in 1530 but not before constructing some picturesque gardens: Bagh-i Vafa in Kabul (the Garden of Fidelity, 1508), the Bagh-i-Kilan near Kabul, and the Araam Bagh (the Garden of Rest, 1528) and the Zuhara Bagh, both in Agra.

The general characteristics of a Mughal garden as identified by C.M. Villiers Stuart in her book, *Gardens of the Great Mughals*, can

Above: An aerial view of the tomb of Itmad-al-Daula revealing the strict adherence to symmetry in both the landscape and the architecture of the period.

be broadly summarized as being derivatives of the great garden traditions of Persia and Turkistan and invariably being either square or rectangular in shape. They were further divided into smaller subdivisions or parterres that were filled with fruit trees and flowers. In fact, gardeners were brought from Persia to tend these gardens and many exotic plants and flowers were grown successfully.

Larger trees defined the main axis of the garden, stretching along the perimeter walls. The gardens, in keeping with the Islamic notion of a Paradise garden, were almost always enclosed by high walls pierced by imposing gates, with some of the larger gardens featuring gates on all four sides.

Water played a very important role in the layout of these gardens, both for its use in irrigation as well as for its cooling effect during the hot summer months. Typically, water would run down a trim stone or a brick-edged canal, falling from one level to another in smooth cascades or 'rushing down as a furious white foam over carved water chutes'. The water from these canals would then flow into a larger tank (hauz), sometimes decorated with fountains.

The pavilions intended for both leisure and relaxation were usually

placed in the centre of the largest of these pools and served as a retreat from the sun. In addition, the larger gardens had canals running along their lengths, terminating in baradaris (buildings or rooms with twelve doors). Typically, a large masonry platform was built under a tree and served as the venue for entertainment, where the emperor and his courtiers would listen to musical recitals and poetry.

In his memoirs written in his native Turki, Emperor Babur describes at length the Bagh-i Vafa (the Garden of Fidelity):

Opposite the fort of Adinahpur, to the south, on a rising ground, I formed a char-bagh in the year 1508. It is called Bagh-i Vafa. It overlooks the river, which flows between the fort and the palace. In the year in which I defeated Behar Khan and conquered Lahore and Dibalpur, I brought plants and planted them here. They grew and thrived. The year before I had also planted sugarcane in it, which thrived remarkably well. I sent some of them to Badakhshan and

Above: This delicate drawing shows Muhammad Shah on horseback surveying his gardens.

Bokhara. It is on an elevated site and enjoys running water, and the climate in the winter season is temperate. In the garden there is a small hillock, from which a stream of water, sufficient to drive a mill, incessantly flows into the garden below. The four-fold plot of the garden is situated on this eminence. On the southwest part of this garden is a reservoir of water twenty feet square, which is wholly planted with orange trees; there are likewise pomegranates. All around the piece of water the ground is quite covered with clover. This spot is the very eye of the beauty of the garden. At the time the oranges become yellow, the prospect is delightful. Indeed the garden is charmingly laid out. To the south of this garden lies the Koh-i Sefid (the White Mountain of Nangenhar). There is no road by which one can pass it on horseback.[2]

A court painting by the portrait painter of the Mughal court, Bishandas, shows Babur along with his architect laying out a *charbagh* garden. Interestingly, all the components that came to characterize Mughal gardens are represented here. An essentially square garden, surrounded by high walls with fruit trees along the perimeter, a four-fold subdivision with individual parterres delineated by water channels (representing the four rivers of life) and culminating in a tank or *hauz* are all portrayed in the painting. Workers are shown using a measuring tape to ensure exactitude in the laying out of the garden.

An innate love of nature coupled with an essentially nomadic lifestyle would have made Babur, acclimatized to a rough life in the Hindu Kush mountains, very much at home in gardens such as this. A series of tents erected in such a space would quite conceivably be the emperor's idea of home. The topmost terrace also known as the *zenana* was the reserve of women, who could see the gardens below from the privacy of their quarters. While subsequent building projects replaced cloth (tents) as the dominant building material with sandstone and marble, Mughal architecture continued to retain the pavilion and tent-like style.[3]

Above: Rani Sisodia Bagh, Jaipur, Rajasthan.

Empress Nur Jahan is seen here relaxing with her husband Jehangir and Prince Khurram in what is widely believed to be the Ram Bagh. Nur Jahan remodelled this garden in 1621.

Facing Page: The Chowmahalla Palace, photographed by Deen Dayal in the 1880s, was the seat of the Asaf Jahi dynasty and later became the official residence of the Nizam of Hyderabad. Its construction began in 1750 by Salabat Jung and was completed between 1857 and 1869. Originally set in forty-five acres of land, a northern courtyard with a large central pool and a southern courtyard, around which four palaces – Afzal Mahal, Mahtab Mahal, Tahniyat Mahal and Aftab Mahal – are located, spatially organize the complex. While the northern courtyard is built in a Neoclassical style, the northern courtyard has both Persian elements and ornate stucco work.

After the battle of Panipat in 1526, Babur visited Agra with a view to establish a garden in the Persian tradition that he was familiar with. Unfortunately for him, the beautiful sites to be found either in the hills of Kabul or in Samarkand were absent in the dusty plains of Agra. An astute planter, he noted that the Hindu population had largely lost interest in the art of garden design. Their gardens, according to him, were now essentially a grove of trees surrounding a tank that was used as water catchment area. What struck Babur immediately was the importance of artificial means of irrigation for his gardens. He lamented: 'One of the great defects of Hindustan is its lack of flowing water . . . water by means of wheels should be made to flow wherever I might settle down . . . grounds should be laid in an orderly and symmetrical way.' [4]

Describing his angst at the time and subsequent course of action, he wrote:

Shortly after coming to Agra, I passed the Jumna (Yamuna) with this object in view, and examined the country, to pitch upon a fit spot for a garden. The whole was so ugly and detestable, that I re-passed the river quite repulsed and

disgusted. In consequence of the want of beauty and the disagreeable aspect of the country, I gave up my intention of making a *char-bagh*; but as no better situation presented itself near Agra, I was finally compelled to make the best of this same spot. First of all I began to sink the large well which supplies the baths with water; I next fell to work on the piece of ground on which are the *ambli* (Indian tamarind trees), and the octagonal tank and its enclosure; and afterwards the tank and *talar*, or grand hall of audience, that are in front of the stone palace. I next finished the garden of the private apartments, and the apartments themselves, after which I completed the baths. In this way, going on, without neatness and order, in the Hindu fashion, I, however, produced edifices and gardens which possessed considerable regularity. In every corner I planted suitable gardens; in every garden I sowed roses and narcissus regularly, and in beds corresponding to each other. We were annoyed with three things in Hindustan: one was the heat, another its strong winds, the third its dust. Baths were the means of

removing all three inconveniences. In the bath we could not be affected by the winds. During the hot winds, the cold can there be rendered so intense, that a person often feels as if quite powerless from it. The room of the bath, in which is the tub or cistern, is finished wholly of stone. The water-run is of white stone: all the rest of it, its floor and roof, is of red sandstone, which is the stone of Biana. Khalifeh, Sheikh Zin, Yunis Ali and several others, who procured situations on the banks of the river, made regular and elegant gardens and tanks, and constructed wheels after the fashion of Lahore and Dibalpur, by means of which they procured a supply of water. The men of Hind, who had never before seen places formed on such a plan, or laid out with so much elegance, gave the name Kabul to the side of the Jumna on which these palaces were built.[5]

Interestingly, in spite of his initial disdain for the ugly sites, an inadequate water supply and the heat of the plains, Babur felt the need to embark on his garden project. Realizing that the only way to sustain such an endeavour would be to first build large tanks for

the collection and storage of water, Babur astutely did so, demonstrating his desire to harness whatever little natural resources were available to him and to bring to the Indian subcontinent the notion of a Paradise garden along the lines of what would have been found in Persia.

Also of note was the need to construct an ordered view of the world ('edifices and gardens . . . possessed of considerable regularity'), a view informed by the restriction in Islam to depict either human beings or animals in images, resulting in the development of intricate floral and geometrical patterns (the rigid geometry associated with the *char-bagh*, in contrast to the 'natural' appearance of the English country garden).

Ram Bagh, the garden probably being referred to by Babur in his description, was in contrast to the gardens of Sikandra. Ram Bagh was essentially an Islamic garden, based on the precedents to be found in Persia and Kabul. Probably the first garden to be created in India by Babur, it heralded a spectacular series of Mughal gardens in India.

Emperor Akbar's Tomb at Sikandra and its adjoining gardens were, in contrast, not based on Islamic precedents alone but were an amalgamation of outside influences. Throughout his life and reign, Akbar was a secular leader, abolishing *jizya*, the tax on non-Muslims, and establishing the Din-i-Ilahi, a new faith, a synthesis of religions that drew on the teachings of Islam, Hinduism, Christianity and Zororastrianism.[6]

The tomb, set in 119 acres of land, is aligned along the four cardinal points and while it was started by Akbar in 1600, it was his son Jehangir who completed it (1605-13). While the gardens surrounding the tomb are modelled on those around Humayun's Tomb in Delhi, the resting place of Akbar manifests a different architectural style.

Aligned more closely to buildings that follow a traditional palace typology, the mausoleum in Agra, with its five storeys and

Above: The formal gardens at Laxmi Vilas Palace, designed by William Goldring in 1900, included a sculpture garden within the palace grounds.

upper-level courtyard does not have a stylistic allegiance to Humayun's domed tomb but does share common features, as Catherine Asher points out, with other contemporary works such as the tomb of Shah Begum and the earlier multi-storeyed tomb of Muhammand Ghaus in Gwalior, with its *chhatris* (canopies). Nor can one easily ignore the influence of such structures as the Panch Mahal or the Diwan-i-Khas in nearby Fatehpur Sikri.[7]

The departure that we see from the Timurid traditions of Akbar's ancestors to one that is more closely associated with the influences of the religious landscape around him and the subsequent indigenization of his architecture is evidence that the emperor saw himself as a uniting force in the subcontinent as against being merely an invader. By integrating elements of both Hindu and Islamic architecture in the design of his palaces and tombs, Akbar used architecture and landscape as vehicles to establish continuity with his Timurid past, while encompassing the collective identities of the heterogenous people of India through the use of architectural elements that were familiar to them.

Before we examine these two buildings in greater detail it would be important to look at how these works would have been perceived by visitors. Both Humayun and Akbar used architecture as a means not only to communicate a broader worldview but also to establish the context of their administration and rule.

Philosophers and cultural theorists have written extensively about the representation of a work and the relationship between an author and a text, and that between a reader and a text. Structuralism, the branch of philosophy which espouses a view that each element is determined and defined by its relationship to other elements (with an external element serving as a catalyst that calls it into being), and a Deconstructivist reading that argues (as distinct from a Structuralist view) that nothing stands outside a system of dependencies as systems interact with systems, would help serve as theoretical constructs from which to form an understanding of the potency of a building such as Humayun's Tomb.

Above: Formal, walled gardens extend before the Bashi Bagh Palace in Hyderabad.

As D. Fairchild Ruggles accurately states in his article, 'Humayun's Tomb and Garden: Typologies and Visual Order': 'the power of vision has been recognized and politically manipulated in both the European and Islamic contexts; but in Islam, image-making and the power of vision are more sensitive issues, so much so that they are historically controlled and sometimes even suppressed.' He adds, 'in pre-modern Islamic society the gaze was curtailed by the veiling and clothing of the body, [so] in architecture, doors, screens, and even walls limited vision to select individuals; and even in urban space, there were few occasions when space was opened up by an avenue or plaza to "reveal" the city.'[8]

'Image-making' and the 'power of vision' that Ruggles writes about presupposes a receptive audience that engages the 'power of vision' as a tool to create a sense-perceptive understanding of the spatial and visual relationships between themselves and in the greater environment.

However, when considered from the perspective of patronage and intent, the heterogeneity that constituted Mughal subjects (demographically as diverse as Timurid, Muslim, Hindu, Jain and Buddhist people), coupled with the fact that the Mughals were an invading force, would have made it politically imperative to commission works of art and architecture that would give structure to an otherwise ethnically disparate and socially complex populace. The gardens and architecture alike were to be a binding force.

Both architecture and landscape design are more closely aligned to the performing arts than the visual arts. The multiple and infinite perspectives from which these works are perceived, a function of the viewer 'residing' in them, makes them particularly appropriate as a stage for the enactment of public ceremonies.[9]

The transformation of a garden, tomb or pavilion into a theatrical set from which symbolism and representation are perceived, not in terms of that which is visually manifest but in its 'effect on' and

accompanying 'associations with' was of paramount importance.

Designed to impress the laity, monuments such as Humayun's Tomb often had an elaborate sequence of entrance. A large wall encases the grounds of Humayun's Tomb, creating a sense of heightened anticipation as one catches the first view. Seen from a distance, the tomb's great size becomes all the more apparent as one traverses the *char-bagh* through the various orchestrated subdivisions before climbing up to the plinth through a narrow flight of steps.

The model for subsequent tomb gardens, the concept for the layout in the *char-bagh* style was initiated by Humayun's widow, Haji Begum. The tomb itself is based on a *hasht-bihisht* (eight paradises) plan, one that the Mughals derived from earlier Timurid buildings, such as Subz Burj and the Nila Gumbad in Delhi. Other examples of this plan that they would have been familiar with are the *khanaqah* (dwelling made for a Sufi saint) of Shaykh Armani in

Deh-i Minar, southwest of Herat, and also the *khanaqah* of Qasim Shaykh at Kermin, northeast of Bukhara.

The plan consists of a central square or rectangular chamber with its corners either braced with towers or more commonly chamfered to form an octagon with smaller chambers opening out from it, making it radially symmetrical. From the octagonal centre (referred to as *muthamman baghdadi* by the Mughals), *pishtaqs* (flat-roofed verandas) are located centrally on the squared-off outer flanks. The combined figure forms a nine-part division.

In Humayun's Tomb, the architects, Sayyid Muhammad and his father, Mirak Sayyid Ghiyath, composed the plan to incorporate four such octagonal forms at the corners of the centrally located larger octagon. Diagonal corridors then interlinked each of these octagons.

Seen here are a watercolour and ink drawing of Akbar's Tomb at Sikandra (left) and an aerial photograph of the tomb (above).

The relatively recently (1968) constructed Lodhi Garden by J.A. Stein and Garrett Eckbo surrounds monuments of the Sayyid and Lodhi dynasties.

The architects achieved a very high level of complexity by the geometric manipulation and arrangement of four similar octagonal elements around a larger central one.

The *hasht-bihisht* plan was not restricted to mausoleums and can also be found in *khanaqahs*. While one can speculate about the correlation between a home for the dead and a home for the living, the typological interchangeability[10] that is evident here is also prevalent in the relationship between tomb and garden as well as pavilion and garden. Formally, both these structures are very similar yet, as Ruggles points out, their optical ordering has dissimilar effects.

Humayun's Tomb in Delhi was completed in 1571. It is here that the first example of a cross-axial garden in India can be seen. The tomb is made of red sandstone (reminding one of the royal red tents that Humayun's ancestors would have used) and white marble. The double-domed structure is built on a high plinth that is centrally located in the *char-bagh*. *Khiyabans* or paved walkways that divide the garden into its four parts terminate in gate houses or other such secondary structures. This relationship between building and garden was to reappear decades later in the tomb of Itimad-ud-Daula in Agra (1626-28) and then again at the Taj Mahal, also in Agra (1632-43). Ruggles attributes this to the development of a new dynastic tomb type.[11] The plinth consists of 124 vaulted chambers over which the *hasht-bihisht* tomb rests.

Glenn Lowry in his article argues that Akbar, who completed the tomb, attempted to both establish his Timurid lineage as well as his commitment to the Indian subcontinent where his future lay. The plan and the bulbous dome recalled earlier Timurid architectural traditions while the indigenous red sandstone and white marble were grounded firmly in the material palette of his new homeland.[12] An interesting analysis by Fairchild Ruggles of Humayun's Tomb describes the manner in which optical ordering and perception alters the relationship between the garden and pavilion or tomb and thereby alters both its symbolism and meaning.

In palace gardens, for example, Ruggles states that the hierarchy of the axes and the points of intersection in the formal layout of the complexes serves the purposes of both the king and the institution.

Above: The circular or Butterfly Garden at Rashtrapati Bhawan (the Presidential Palace). The gardens in their entirety are referred to as the Mughal Garden, after having been modelled after such a historical precedent.

For example, the location of the pavilion marks the position around which the garden is organized and to be seen. From the pavilion, the garden is viewed, a place that would otherwise have been reserved for the king and by extension, represents him in his physical absence.

The article, however, distinguishes between the role played by palace gardens and funerary gardens, in which the role of the object being viewed and the viewer is reversed. The tomb becomes the object and the garden is a mere setting through which the ritual of circumambulation (*tawaf*) is enacted.

While it is evident that the architectural and spatial relationships between the pavilion and garden, and tomb and garden are similar, the point of distinction lies in the experience of the viewer and the effect it has on them. For example, at the Shalimar Gardens in Srinagar, Kashmir, a tripartite terraced division delineates the outer, the middle and the upper gardens.

With each successive terrace encompassing a greater level of privacy and empowerment, it focuses the 'gaze' and directs it towards the gardens, making the 'centre point both unique and empowering; the surrounding space diffused and dependent'. As one might imagine, the potency of such a position is matched only by the prime actor in the set, the emperor or the empress. It is immaterial whether such a pavilion is placed physically in the centre of the composition or is in the optical centre.

The Shalimar Bagh, measuring 540 metres by 244 metres, is large and imposing, set as it is against the backdrop of the Pir Panjal mountains. A spring feeds water to a central canal, bisecting the garden along its length and forming the primary axis.

The site was converted into a Mughal garden in 1620 with Jehangir asking his son Shah Jahan to dam a nearby stream. In 1634, the garden was then further enlarged to reach the foothills of the mountains. The Mughals referred to these gardens as Bagh-i Faiz Baksh and Farah Baksh. The lower garden, Farah Baksh (Bestower of Pleasure) features a pavilion, the Diwan-i-Am (Hall of Public Audience) and the upper garden or Bagh-i Faiz Baksh (Bestower of Plenty) was meant for private use.

With carved water chutes and niches for evening illumination, fountains further embellish the gardens. A pavilion marks the

Above: A waterfall in the Shalimar Bagh in Srinagar.

Following pages: A view of Humayun's Tomb with its recently restored *char-bagh* and surrounding walls.

centre of each garden and in the centre of the Farah Baksh, a black platform, with its tiered roof, served as the emperor's throne.

In palace gardens such as those in Srinagar, a visitor can for a moment assume a 'position of primacy' by occupying that privileged position and gazing down the central vista. The terraces unfold successively below the gardens, and the view from the pavilion displays a formal composition of the gardens that is at once linear and hierachial. Today, the visitor can view the garden from where the emperor would have, and from there see the stepped terraces and the strong axiality.

The formal geometry of the garden, its axiality, and the ordering of the spaces instil a sense of empowerment in the viewer, acting as a reminder that it was the sole preserve of the emperor.

In a tomb garden, on the contrary, the position of primacy is not coveted at all. It is the space of the dead and, while in a palace garden the axis and the spatial disposition contribute towards emphasizing the institution of royalty, here a barrier screen, or *hizar*, make the sarcophagus the object of the gaze as one looks at it rather than from it. The role of the garden with the tomb within it is thus a commemoration of the dead and establishes historical lineage.[13]

Lisa Golombek's study of Gazur Gah, a shrine near Herat traces the use of a *hizar* screen in a funerary context and states that it was originally intended to designate an open-air burial ground. According to her study, the Prophet's burial place in Medina is marked both by an enclosing screen as well as a tomb.[14] The purpose of the screen is symbolic and while it visually concealed the sarcophagus, it was opened, as François Bernier describes when he visited the Taj Mahal, 'with much ceremony once in a year and once only' and that Christians were not allowed to enter it.[15]

To further accentuate the difference between the sanctimony of the space of the dead and the ability to appropriate, even if temporarily,

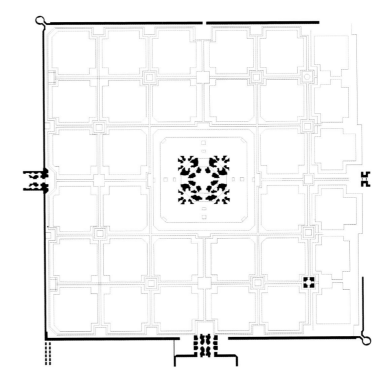

Above: Schematic plan of Humayun's Tomb in New Delhi.

Facing page: Humayun's Tomb, New Delhi, was built on orders from Hamida Banu Begum. Construction began in 1562. The architect reportedly was Sayyed Muhammad ibn Mirak Ghiyathuddin along with his father Mirak Ghiyathuddin. It took eight years to build and was constructed in the midst of a *char-bagh* garden.

the position of the king, Mughal tombs almost always placed a cenotaph with a crypt lying directly below it, thus excluding the possibility of anyone ever standing at the point of axial intersection. Symbolically, as Ruggles points out, the occupant, 'cannot be displaced; he is again both present in (body) and absent (in death) even more so than in the garden pavilion because the temporal frame of the tomb is eternity. The garden is about sovereignty, and the mausoleum is about dynasty. When the mausoleum is implanted in a garden, as it is at Humayun's Tomb, sovereignty and dynasty are combined in a teleological statement that the king is the king as he always has been and always will be.'[16]

Located not too far from the Shalimar Gardens in Srinagar is Nishat Bagh, the Garden of Gladness. Designed by Yamim-al Daula Asaf Khan, these gardens are spread across twelve terraces that ascend the mountainside. Built by Asaf Khan, Shah Jahan's prime minister and father-in-law, the gardens, unlike those at Shalimar are not royal pleasure gardens, but residential gardens, intended to be accessed directly from the Dal lake. (A road constructed along the perimeter of the lake has subsequently altered the original sequence of entrance).

With flowers as varied as a roses, lilies and geraniums and trees such as chinars, cypresses and a variety of fruit-bearing ones, Nishat Bagh was the pride of Asaf Khan. While the *zenana* is enclosed by an eighteen-foot-high wall that runs along the width of the garden, stone and marble statues mark the numerous fountains and waterfalls that dot the terraces. The *baradari* so characteristic of gardens of this type is on the third terrace. Measuring fifty-nine feet long and forty-eight feet wide, it is flanked by wooden latticed windows. Its harmonious integration with the mountain slopes and its numerous terraces, waterbodies and trees made this a much coveted garden, so much so that it is believed that Shah Jahan on not being offered it by his father-in-law, the *wazir*, ordered its supply of water to be cut off![17]

Above: Winter at the Shalimar Gardens in Srinagar. Originally called Farah Baksh or The Delightful, Shalimar Bagh was built by Mughal Emperor Jehangir in 1616 and then subsequently a second garden, Faiz Baksh, The Bountiful, was added later by Shah Jahan. The garden covers an area of approximately 12.4 hectares.

Shah Jahan, as a builder, is undoubtedly best known for the mausoleum he constructed, the Taj Mahal (1630), for his wife Mumtaz Mahal. The gardens are set within a large 300-metre square boundary in the *char-bagh* typology that is characteristic of Mughal gardens. A raised marble-lined water tank called Hawd al-Kawthar is located centrally between the main gate and the tomb, mirroring the mausoleum in all its glory.

Distinguishing itself from Humayun's Tomb, the Taj Mahal is located not in the midst of its gardens but at the end of the north-south axis, along the banks of the Yamuna. The mausoleum, by virtue of its location when accessed from the landlocked south gateways, serves as the terminal point in the composition.

Across the river, to the north, lies what was the Mehtab Bagh or the Moonlight Garden. Originally spread over twenty-five acres, the garden were once filled with pavilions, fountains, reflecting pools and fragrant flowers.

The garden is a four-quartered, *char-bagh* garden, rectilinear and symmetrical. While a number of Mughal garden designs had to be forfeited in keeping with the Indian landscape, an idea that endured was the creation of gardens adjoining waterbodies, particularly rivers. (This is also evident in the gardens of Kashmir where they were originally entered from the Dal lake).

Interestingly, as originally conceived, the Taj Mahal would have been situated in the middle of a large garden complex, spanning across the river Yamuna and on to the northern bank, making the river 'a water channel', bisecting the composition. As it had been for his forefathers, Shah Jahan's desire to bring order to an otherwise natural landscape, to demonstrate his ability to administer a large kingdom, is amply evident in both the design and the construction of this tomb.

Above: Fountains from the royal springs of Chasma Shahi. Nestled in the hills above Dal lake, much smaller than its neighbours Shalimar Bagh and Nishat Bagh, Chasma Shahi is nevertheless equally charming and potent.

Following pages: An aerial view of Akbar's Tomb at Sikandra illustrates the influence of both Mughal and Hindu precedents.

نقشه مقبره نواب صفدر جنگ

At the outset, unlike his ancestors, Shah Jahan used the river as a vital, integral part in the overall composition. Mehtab Bagh, a pleasure garden was thus united through river and tomb with the mausoleum's garden, giving the Taj Mahal a centricity that at first is not immediately apparent.

Viewed first from the south entrance gateway, the white-marbled tomb glistens in formidable splendour. Entered first through a forecourt, the *jilaukhana*, and then through the *darwaz-i-rauza*, the tomb sits on a large marble plinth that is ninety-three metres long. A river-front terrace in turn supports this plinth. Flanked on the west by a red sandstone mosque crowned by a large white marble dome and on the east by a nearly identical structure, which in contemporary texts had been referred to as a guest house or *mehman khana*, the Taj Mahal rises majestically above the gardens.

While numerous artisans worked on the design and subsequent construction of this funerary complex, contemporary sources identify Makramat Khan (who later supervised the construction of Shahjahanabad) and Abd al-Karim (a master architect during Jehangir's reign and also responsible for the Shah Burj in Lahore Fort) as the supervisors of the project. The poet Lutf Allah, identifies his father, Ustad Ahmad Lahauri as the designer of the tomb, while Amanat Khan is credited as being the calligrapher.[18] Catherine Asher in her book speculates that Emperor Shah Jahan too played an integral role in the design of the tomb, but his name has been omitted from the official chronicle written by Lahauri.[19]

Hodgson's Plan of 1799 is perhaps the earliest known survey of the Taj Mahal complex and shows both the buildings and the plantations conforming to a grid that extended from Taj Ganj to Mehtab Bagh. Interestingly, as Priyaleen Singh in her article 'From Paradise to Picturesque' accurately describes, with colonialism came both new ideologies and aesthetic orientations that were captured and communicated through the works of artists such as

Above: A partial view of Akbar's Tomb in Sikandra, with a centrally located water channel that alludes to a *char-bagh* garden design.

William Hodges and the Daniells. Works such as 'Picturesque tour along the river Ganges and Jamuna in India' by Charles Forrest, and 'Views in the Himalaya Mountains' by James Baillie Fraser portrayed architectural ruins that served as 'follies' (whimsical or extravagant structures built to serve as a conversation piece that lend interest to a view or commemorate a person or event) within what were now English-style gardens.[20] The Taj Mahal funerary complex was no exception.

With the establishment of the Archaeological Survey of India (ASI) in 1862, British engineers who at the time were at the helm of the institution, followed manuals prepared by the Agricultural and Horticultural Societies in forming a landscaping strategy. The ASI was at the time charged by other prerogatives that often neglected the cultural, aesthetic and sociological considerations that had led to the formation of these monuments and gardens. In fact, the gardens of the Taj Mahal were used as a favourite resort for Agra's cantonments with a regimental band playing on the mausoleum's terraces! It was, as Singh further points out in her

paper, also used for picnics, moonlight parties, morning walks and even sports on the terraces! The Mehtab Bagh was described as 'elegant camping grounds'. The gardens of the Taj Mahal that we have inherited today are thus no more than 'a post-colonial interpretation of a colonial intervention in a Mughal Garden'.[21]

While this statement is descriptively accurate, it nonetheless indicates an inevitable process of evolution. The synthesis and amalgamation of Timurid and Hindu traditions was both inevitable and desirable. The influence of the British colonizers may have

Above: A colour lithograph of the Taj Mahal viewed from its gardens by Thomas and William Daniell.

Following pages: (108-109) A view of the Taj Mahal that portrays not only its strong axiality and symmetry but also the key role played by the impeccably laid-out gardens in the overall composition. Barely visible as a sliver behind the Taj Mahal is the river Yamuna, across the banks of which was to be the Mehtab Bagh. (110-111) A view from above the dome of the Taj Mahal looking towards the gardens and entrance pavilion.

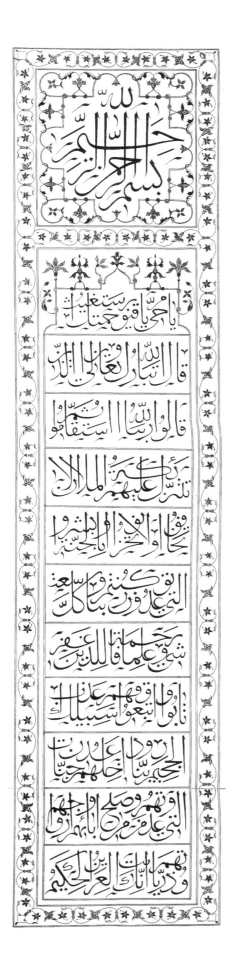

bastardized works when viewed as stagnant constructs but nevertheless played their role in the evolution of buildings and gardens. Through a process of representation, whether visual or textual, it established an interpretive and theoretical agenda that helped inform ideas on garden and landscape design.

While the Taj Mahal, along with Humayun's Tomb, undoubtedly represents the more renowned examples of tomb gardens, other Mughal gardens are also worthy of mention.

Fadai Khan, the foster brother of the cunning Mughal emperor Aurangzeb, built the seventeenth-century gardens at Pinjore. Watered by the holy spring of Panchpura, the terraced gardens served the purposes of both defence and pleasure.[22] A keen builder, Fadai Khan supervised the construction of the great mosque in Lahore and was thus probably excited at the potential of the new site with its natural water spring.

Built in the *char-bagh* tradition, the gardens at Pinjore are characterized by three structures: the Rang Mahal (painted palace), the Sheesh Mahal (glass palace), and the Jal Mahal (water palace). The gardens are distinguished from their predecessors by the approach from the uppermost terrace before they traverse down along the central canal to the lower terraces.

Unlike the great gardens of Kashmir, which were approached originally by boat from the Dal lake, the gardens at Pinjore are accessed rather unceremoniously through a winding road. However, the presence of a natural spring that provided a constant source of clear and clean water more than made up for its rather humble entrance. Fadai Khan's use of precious water for gardening and

Left: Ornate calligraphic inscriptions along with floral motifs such as this embellish the cenotaph of Mumtaz Mahal at the Taj Mahal. Highly skilled artisans and craftsman toiled unrellentessly to produce the exquisite inlay work.

Facing Page Left: A historic eighteenth century plan of the Taj Mahal complex prepared by Thomas and William Daniell. The symmetry associated with the gardens and the tomb compliment each other, producing a complex that continues to attract tourists and scholars alike.
Right: A recent aerial photograph of the Taj Mahal Complex, illustrating not only the survival of the Char Bagh composition but also the effects of urbanization in the immediate vicinity of the mausoleum.

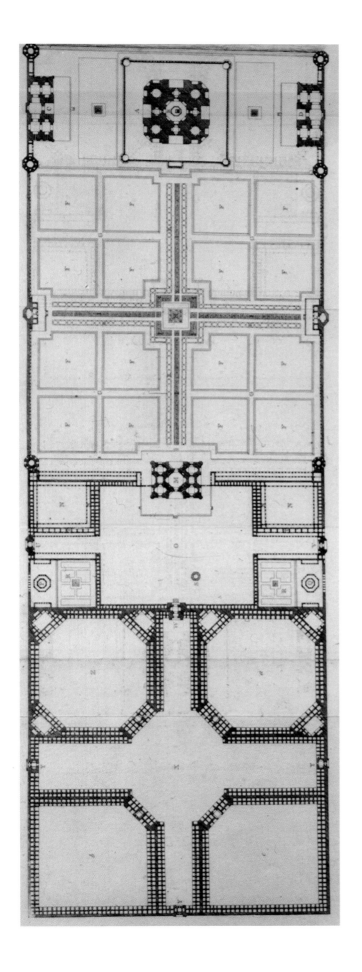

This photograph of the gardens and the buildings of the Deeg Palace are reminiscent of the Mughal architecture and yet have a distinctive flavour as a result of the Jats own aesthetic vision. The royal palace complex is planned along the periphery of the central garden and is flanked by two reservoirs the Rup Sagar on the east and the Gopal Sagar on the west. The finely proportioned halls and arcades coupled with the formality of the Mughal Char Bagh gardens characterize the Jat architecture and gardens of the period.

pleasure seemed extravagant to the rajas of the neighbouring hill states, as Villiers Stuart in her book describes:

A quaint story still survives, how, when at length the work was finished, and Fadai came in state to spend his first summer there, his enjoyment of the garden and its beauties was short-lived; for the Rajas quickly frightened him away. In the districts round Pinjore, and in fact all along the foot of the Himalayas, occasional cases of goitre are to be seen; so from far and wide these poor people were collected by the wily Brahmins, and produced as the ordinary inhabitants of the place. The gardeners all suffered from goitre; every coolie had this dreadful complaint; even the countrywomen carrying up the big flat baskets of fruits and flowers to the zenana terraces were equally disfigured. The ladies of the harem naturally were horrified; it was bad enough to be brought into these wild outlandish jungles, without this new and added terror. For the poor coolie women, well instructed beforehand, had told how the air and water of Pinjore caused this disease, which no one who lived there long ever escaped. A panic reigned in the *zenana*; its inmates implored to be removed at once from such a danger; and finally, Fadai Khan had to give way, and take his ladies to some other place less threatening to their beauty. Had it been the terrible Emperor himself instead of his foster-brother, the cunning Rajas would have met their match. But Fadai Khan, thoroughly deceived, rarely came back to visit his lovely gardens, and the Rajas and their fields were left in peace for a time.[23]

Fadai Khan and Pinjore represent the last of the great Mughal

gardens, a tradition that was brought to India by Babur centuries earlier. With perhaps the exception of the garden palace at Deeg near the Bharatpur bird sanctuary in Rajasthan, where on a perfectly flat site in the midst of a lake, a garden full of parterres, fountains and water courses still exists as a continuation of the Mughal *char-bagh* tradition.

Commenced in 1725, the gardens at the Deeg Palace were the greatest artistic accomplishment of the Hindu king, Surajmal, the son of the Jat ruler, Badan Singh, who founded the Jat house of Bharatpur. While the palace in part is characterized by a series of monuments within it, what distinguishes it is the garden that has been laid out with both rigour and exactitude. James Ferguson, in fact, commented on it stating that it had 'a regularity which would satisfy the most fastidious Renaissance architect'.[24]

Above: Built by Asaf-ud-daulah, the Nawab of Lucknow in 1784, the Bara Imambara is a shrine for Shiite Muslims to congregate and observe Muharram. The step-well or *baoli*, an element associated more closely with Hindu architecture, is the defining feature in the expansive lawns. The commission was awarded on the basis of an architectural competition; the winning architect, Kifayatullah was buried in the main hall alongside his patron.

Following pages: The ornamental garden and accompanying tile work at the entrance court of the luxurious Udai Vilas Hotel on the banks of Lake Pichola in Udaipur, Rajasthan, serves as a prelude to the exclusively landscaped thirty-acre property.

Built by Maharaja Ganga Singh in 1902 in memory of his father Maharaja Lal Singhji, this imposing red sandstone palace was designed by Col. Sir Swinton Jacob in what can broadly be referred to as the Indo-Saracenic style. Sprawling lawns with dancing peacocks and bougainvilleas transform the desert landscape.

A BRIEF HISTORY OF GARDEN STYLES

Above: Aerial view of the Amboise city and castle, located on the banks of the Loire river. The Loire Valley, known as the Garden of France, has over 120 gardens and parks.

Top: Parterre garden, Villa Lante, Italy.

A number of garden styles have developed over the centuries throughout the world. Responding to both the specificity of an immediate need as well as for the sheer pleasure derived from them, gardens of great variety and skill can be found in almost everywhere. As might be imagined, with growing trade and developing communication networks, a cross-pollination of ideas was inevitable. The gardens of India too, were not insulated from this process and have been much enriched by it. Listed below are a few predominantly European garden styles, some of which have had a direct influence on Indian gardens.

Temple Gardens

Originally used solely by pharaohs and priests, the oldest temple gardens can be found in Egypt. Generally open to the public on festival days, these gardens were not only spaces used for congregations, but their sacred groves were sought after for their tranquillity and quiet isolation, conducive to meditation. The gardens themselves often featured large water bodies, fruit-bearing trees as well as flower and vegetable gardens.

Sacred Groves

The wooded areas associated with ancient Egyptian temples became refuges from the congestion of cities. If there was a source of water, it became a natural place for an altar or a temple. Often these spaces were also used for discourse, education and in the case of the ancient Greeks, exercise too.

The Courtyard

Enclosed by walls on all sides, courtyards developed as a means of enjoying outdoor spaces within the greater confines of a built

The ornamental gardens of Chateau d'Angers in France abut the seventeen towers, work on which was completed in 1240.

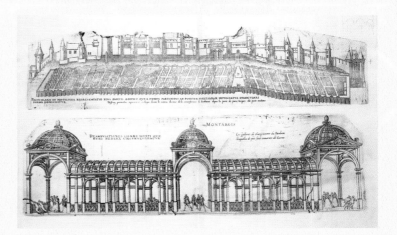

Above: The aerial view of La Petraia, an erstwhile Medici villa, shows the formal gardens with their parterres and accompanying terraces set against the villa and a dense grove of trees in the background.

Top: 'Views of Montargis' – published in the 1570s, in the engravings collection, 'Les Plus Belles Batiments de France' – depicts the early integration of architecture and gardens.

environment. Secure, private and intimate, like the Egyptian domestic garden, these spaces were used for entertaining, growing plants and living amid nature. Courtyards helped to keep people cool in the summer and warm in the winter.

Broadly speaking, courtyards, depending on their scale, fall into two categories.

An atrium: Generally located in the centre of a dwelling unit, it was used primarily to provide light, ventilation and a clear internal circulation route to the unit. It was constructed below the ground level by a couple of inches to allow rain water to collect and subsequently drain from it.

A colonnade: Wrapping around the open space and covered at the roof level to form a veranda through which rooms within the house could be accessed, it enclosed an open space often studded with fountains and statues along with flowers, herbs, shrubs and trees.

The Villa

Developed originally in Greece and then adopted as a building type in the Roman empire, the villa soon came to refer to an estate bound by walls and enclosing a number of buildings and different types of gardens. Among the more explicit examples of such structures is Hadrian's Villa (Villa Adriana), built in the second century BC, from where the emperor administered his empire. These structures, as in the case of the Villa Lante, even enclosed hunting parks.

Castle Gardens

Fortifications, such as castles, had gardens for the families of the soldiers who resided in them. Much like the domestic garden, these gardens too were built for private pleasure, although they belonged to the greater collective public. The gardens varied from being either a

Above and Top: The gardens in the Château de Chenonceau, Loire, France.

An avenue of cypress trees with a fountain at the end and a palazzo in the distance in Boboli Gardens, Florence, Italy.

small rectangular enclosure to irregular geometrical shapes. While no examples survive, illustrations of them in medieval prayer books exist, showing them with trellis fencing, lawns, arbours and flowers.

Early Renaissance Style

The renaissance garden developed when people no longer had to live within larger fortifications. Ornamental and picturesque, these gardens were marked by the social dimension of such a space, that is, to entertain friends, hold private discussions and indulge in the private pleasures of home and garden. Like pleasure gardens, these too were designed to be viewed and enjoyed from the upper storeys of a house. Contrary to contemporary developments in the east, the early renaissance gardens had little or no geometrical relationship between house and garden.

High Renaissance Style

Medieval gardens until this point had been introverted, enclosed between walls, the private sanctuary of a select few. The renaissance garden marked a departure from this aspect. Donato Bramante, the renaissance architect, employed a central axis to impose an order in the relationship between house and garden. Steps leading to terraces, alcoves, fountains and niches were placed intermittently off the central axis. Often these spaces housed fruit trees, statues or terracotta pots with flowers.

Mannerist Style

Novelty, allusion and surprise were the characteristics of Mannerist gardens, which broke away from the static formality of their predecessors. Dramatic features entertained people when the

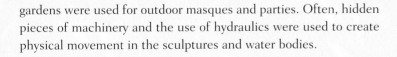

An aerial view of Blenheim Palace, home to the eleventh Duke of Marlborough and the birthplace of Winston Churchill, that is set within 2,100 acres of parkland landscaped by 'Capability' Brown. Sweeping lawns, formal gardens and a beautiful lake surround the Baroque palace.

Above: The park at Harewood House was designed by Lancelot Brown between 1758 and 1772. The terrace was designed as a point of transition between the house and the park.

Top: Kew Gardens is an important botanical research institution with conservatories, a herbarium, an arboretum, a library and a seed bank, among a host of other facilities, set within 300 acres of land.

gardens were used for outdoor masques and parties. Often, hidden pieces of machinery and the use of hydraulics were used to create physical movement in the sculptures and water bodies.

Early Baroque

With the counter-reformation and the desire of the Church to re-establish its authority, early Baroque planning focused on the axis and lines of sight that projected beyond the sole confines of individual gardens. For example, the villas of Frescati had their lines of sight fixed on St Peters in Rome, while Pope Sixtus V envisioned Rome, fixing the vistas on a series of obelisks. A preoccupation with geometry, optics and perspective are all characteristic of this period in garden and architecture development.

High Baroque Style

Baroque gardens were built as expressions of the owner's power and importance. As a result, they were theatrical and drew upon the latest developments in mathematics and science, specifically using Cartesian geometry to bring varied and often distant elements into the composition. Generally, a central building with elaborate parterres, fountains and canals would be characteristic features of these gardens.

Serpentine Style

Deriving its name from the free-flowing curves that give this style definition, the serpentine garden featured a circumferential path that enclosed a central park (one that was often used for grazing animals). A lake and an encircling tree belt contributed to making this type of garden distinct from the more extravagant Baroque gardens.

Picturesque and Gardenesque Styles

Wilderness, along with the beauty of untamed nature, was the genesis of this garden style. The creation of a composed, almost fabricated representation of nature, without using it either for domestic pleasures, social gatherings or hunting, marked a departure from earlier garden styles. When developed as a collection of exotic plants from far-off lands, John Claudius Loudon, landscape and garden designer, invented the term 'gardenesque' to describe it.

Landscape Style

A terraced garden near the front of the house used for domestic pleasure, coupled with a serpentine garden for grazing animals and followed by a nature reserve, was the sequence followed by this style of garden. The use of a foreground, mid-ground and background as a compositional strategy and the simultaneous combination of different garden styles served as a precedent for small compact towns with a protected agricultural area built around them and a larger hinterland beyond.

Arts and Crafts Style

With a growing appreciation for craftsmanship and the joy associated with manual labour, the arts and crafts style perhaps demonstrated for the first time the significant contribution towards the maintenance of a garden by its owner. A growing disillusionment with gardens that borrowed ideas and styles from other countries or historical periods, coupled with a growing discernment in plants, crafts and building materials, led to the popularity of this style.[1]

A bird's eye perspective, as seen from Avenue de Paris, of the Chateau, Gardens and Park of Versailles by Pierre Patel.

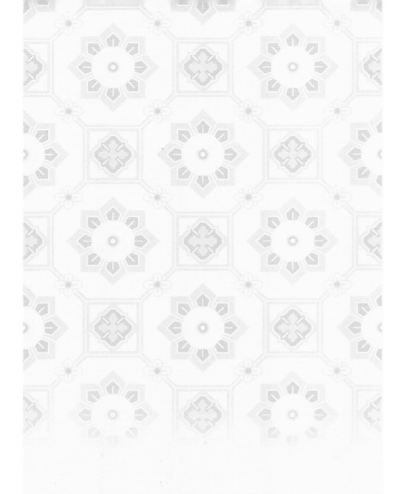

MODERN INDIA
MODERN
LANDSCAPES

View of the formal gardens in front of the Prince of Wales Museum in Mumbai.

With modern India came modern landscapes – as the nature and type of patronage changed considerably, so did the use and specific role that gardens played in the greater cultural landscape. Democracy brought with it its own set of ideals and the programmatic demands of a newly independent nation saw with it the rise of not only new building types but also a set of new themes that broadly formed the conceptual framework within which gardens were conceived and executed.

A couple of themes broadly outline the way gardens and greater landscapes produced in post-Independence India were conceived. These are a sense of history and the desire to create an identity independent of the shadow of the Raj, a 'return' to what has been ill-conceived as a real and true Indian identity. History and historicism, in conjunction with nostalgia, have and will continue to play a defining role in the creation of a collective national identity.

Set in the midst of Said-ul-Ajaib village, next to Delhi's historic Mehrauli area, the twenty-acre Garden of Five Senses was inaugurated in February 2003.

Above: Water channels flanked by gardens at Udai Vilas, Udaipur, flow into a pool with cascading fountains and a sun medallion.

Left: Domed garden pavilions surround the swimming pool at The Oberoi Group's leisure hotel, The Oberoi Rajvilas in Jaipur. Thirty-two acres of landscaped gardens, pavilions and reflecting pools re-create the romance and grandeur of Rajasthan.

Following pages: Mughal Garden at Rashtrapati Bhawan, the Presidential Palace, New Delhi

While highlighting the analytical and image-orientated disposition of a new nation, the gardens designed during this period sought to establish an authentic link to the intricate nuances of a complex and highly developed society, attempting to establish an umbilical relationship with the land within which they were to reside.

Such a strategy is, needless to say, isolating. By representing only particular facets of history and specific periods in an attempt to re-live the zeitgeist or the spirit of a bygone era, the gardens created are at best scenic in nature, adopting through imagery the social structure of a past period. Ironically, the gardens and buildings that history remembers are those of the avant-garde. Alan Colquhoun, in his article entitled 'Three Kinds of Historicism', writes: '. . . in the architectural (and by extension landscape) avant-garde this meant the creation of new forms under the impulse of social and technological development and the symbolic representation of society through these forms.' Their re-creation, in some respects, acknowledges the inability to create a work that captures the spirit of a present time. Both the desire and the need

to do this are important facets in the creation of culture and a type of history that sets itself apart from merely recording the passage of time.

History is a powerful motivator and a concern for tradition is both an important tool and a necessary ingredient for the invention of the future. The artistic practice of using historical forms as a means to associate with a past era through collage (instead of direct imitation) can be an effective tool in its transformation.

Both the gardens at the Palace of Versailles and the Mughal Garden at the Presidential Palace, the Rashtrapati Bhawan in New Delhi, illustrate the manner in which the designers and the architects used historical precedent, innovation and scenographic tact in producing two remarkably different, yet potent gardens.

The initial scheme for the gardens at the Presidential Palace were submitted by Edwin Lansdeer Lutyens to the Government of

Above: An aerial view of the Presidential Palace gardens with the Butterfly Garden in the foreground.

India in 1918. The quadripartite plan, in the tradition of the Mughal *char-bagh* style, was adopted as the dominant motif for its multiple associations. The Mughal Paradise Garden, the Hebrew vision of Eden along with the Hindu *mandala*, drew on the quadripartite plan as a point of departure and was hence adopted by Lutyens as well. Captivated by the potential of water channels and fountains as a means of animating the gardens, Lutyens constructed sixteen-tiered lotus-leaf shaped fountains at the intersections of the two sets of water channels that run from north to south and from east to west.

As both the architect and the landscape architect of the project, Lutyens had the opportunity to seamlessly integrate the building with its surrounding landscape. The lower basement walls extend outwards, enclosing the gardens in a manner similar to those he would have seen on his visits to the Taj Mahal or the Shalimar Gardens in Kashmir and Lahore, recalling the gardens of paradise. The interlocking rectangles of the house plan are further reflected in the parterres of the garden and furthermore, as described by Robert Irving in his book, *Indian Summer*: 'walls and terraces cascade across the landscape in three waves down to the level of the plain, where the tranquillity of a circular pool climaxes in the main urban axis and faintly echoes the War Memorial rotary more than two miles distant.'[1] Two large terraces, ninety-four feet square on the north and the south, rise from a central square garden that is two hundred feet wide.

The gardens of the north and south are characterized by a fountain in the southern court that shoots water skyward from an octagonal pool, the northern court showering water through a perforated pipe to a grotto tank below. Irving comments on the grotto by saying that 'troughs of placid water frame the frothy square basin, as if to assert the triumph of order over tumult in British India'.[2]

The garden follows a highly structured and formal geometry, stemming from the main composition, and a narrow garden, about

Left: Lotus-leaf fountains punctuate the waterworks in Mughal Garden, spatially organizing the gardens. Moulsri trees adjoining the canals are pruned to resemble mushrooms. Various plants in the gardens, among many others, include mogra, motiya, juhi, bougainvillea, and climbing rose, and trees like cypress and China orange.

430 feet long, bisects the flanking grass and clay tennis courts into two. Terminating in the round Butterfly Garden with its sunken pond, the elaborate compositional strategies employed in the Mughal Garden of the Presidential Estate exemplify a relationship with history through the use of scenographic tact (the lotus-shaped fountains, the grotto) in which it aligns itself convincingly with past historical models. This is done in an attempt not to construct a new vision for a country but to ratify the position given to it by political circumstance.

The explicit desire to create a 'Moghol type'[3] garden belies an intent to create a garden that is rooted in the traditions and imagery of a land. However, it does not necessarily intend to either capture or reflect the zeitgeist of the people, but rather of the colonizers' reality and their explicit intentions.

Irving in his book contrasts this garden to the surrounding natural landscape by describing it as, 'The lushness of the Viceregal garden accentuated the inhospitable nature of the surrounding landscape. The patterns of water, colour, and symmetry from Lutyens' hand were in marked contrast to the arid, drab wilderness outside the estate. The formal palace edifice and its geometric garden, juxtaposed against the untamed Delhi Ridge, was meant to be a telling affirmation of power and of the passionate British resolve to bring order to India – tangible proof, to use poet John Davidson's words, of the "ruthless obligation . . . to be despotic for the world's behoof".'[4]

The juxtaposition of the two landscapes was not accidental, nor was the need to plan at such an elaborate scale (the Rashtrapati Bhawan Estate, spread over 335 acres, is the largest presidential

136

residence in the world). The gardens with their meticulous plantations, numerous water bodies and lotus-shaped fountains formed only a fragment of the overall estate that was characterized predominantly by the palace extending to 200,000 square feet, with 340 decorated rooms!

Deyan Sudjic, describing this phenomena in his book, *The Edifice Complex*, writes:

> Every kind of political culture uses architecture for what can, at heart, be understood as rational, pragmatic purposes, even when it is used to make a symbolic point. But when the line between political calculation and psychopathology breaks down, architecture becomes not just as a matter of practical politics, but a fantasy, or a sickness that consumes its victims.

There is a psychological parallel between making a mark on the landscape with a building and the exercise of political power. Both depend on the imposition of will. Certainly, seeing their worldview confirmed by reducing an entire city to the scale of a doll's house in an architectural model has an inherent appeal for those who regard the individual as of no

Connaught Place (now Rajiv Chowk) has a new urban park in its centre, made in tandem with the swank New Delhi Metro which bisects the park from underground: glass panels allow people to peep inside the metro station and a staircase connects the park with it. The park has a central amphitheatre surrounded by fountain pools and gardens, keeping the concentric-circle design of CP intact.

account. Even more attractive is the possibility of imposing their will in the physical sense on a city by re-shaping it in the way that Hausmann did in Paris.[5]

Centuries earlier and continents away, Louis the XIV in Versailles embarked on four building campaigns, in which he invested great effort and time to lay out and transform the elaborate Palace Gardens. Like Lutyens, the project was part of a campaign to establish emphatically and communicate unequivocally the power and reach of the French state. This was nowhere better illustrated than the way Louis the XIV, along with his architect Louis Le Vau, the painter Charles Le Brun and the landscape architect Andre Le Notre, manipulated water channels to create picturesque gardens punctuated by as many as fifty fountains, 620 water-jets, thirty-five kilometres of piping to feed the water-jets and a grand canal with a perimeter of over five kilometres!

With ponds in the immediate vicinity proving inadequate as a means of water supply, supplementary water was provided by nearby ponds. Assisted by gravity, they then fed the fountains. With an increasing number of fountains being commissioned, the architects and engineers had to develop novel ways of capturing the

Above: An old aerial view of the Secretariats and the circular Parliament House.

Facing page: The lush lawns of Imperial Hotel in New Delhi: an oasis in the middle of the city's bustling business district, Connaught Place.

Following pages: The Jantar Mantar Observatory near New Delhi's Connaught Place was built by Maharaja Sawai Jai Singh II in 1724. Four other such observatories were built in Jaipur, Ujjain, Mathura and Varanasi. Sculptural in their manifestation, these astronomical instruments are now part of a public urban park.

Opened in 1921, the Victoria Memorial in Kolkata as seen in this aerial view is located in the midst of sprawling grounds designed by Lord Redesdale and Sir David Prain; the gardens complement the imposing architecture of the building.

Facing page: An illustration of a clearing in a hunting park reveals an oasis emphasizing the importance of water in the gardens in the Palace of Versailles, while obelisk-like hedges engulf visitors in the gardens.

water and recycling water. In 1664, Louis Le Vau designed the Pompe (a water tower built in the north), which was supplied with water from the Clagny pond. The pumps were powered by a combination of horse-power and windmills. By 1671, the Grand Canal was completed and served as a drainage point for the fountains in the garden. The water from here was subsequently pumped to the reservoir on top of the Grotte de Thetys.

With the need for water ever increasing, and the ponds running dry, a new scheme was devised between 1668 and 1674, when water from the Bievre river was diverted to Versailles. The augmented 72,000 cubic metres of water too soon fell short and led to what was perhaps the most ambitious of all his projects, diverting the Seine river to Versailles. Unfortunately, owing to leakages in the conduits and breakdowns in the Machine de Marly (a series of thirty-six-foot-wide water-wheels that moved 221 pumps to transport water 177 yards – 531 feet – up a hillside from the Seine), this was not as successful as originally intended. A final water project that called for the diversion of the Eure river located 160 kilometres south of Versailles, had to be abandoned when the War of the League of Augsburg began. Until then, one-tenth of the military was at work on the project.[6]

Like the Presidential Estate in New Delhi, the scale of the waterworks alone in Versailles demonstrates an 'imposition of will' that is seldom seen. While the analogy between the two estates can extend to include the manner in which the gardens have been landscaped and the use of associative imagery, what is of importance to us is the extent to which the Presidential Estate in New Delhi and the gardens in Versailles sought to impose their worldview. How the re-configuration of a landscape (arguably the greatest historical act) and the extensive use of historical type by the commissioning patrons were utilized to do this, is an interesting study.

The decision to use architecture and more specifically, a garden or landscape design in doing so, is hardly surprising. As a cultural form that has a direct bearing on our lived reality, the choreography of a landscape demonstrates the use of resources that few can aspire to. By virtue of its scale, complexities, the financial and time

resources, along with the necessary horticultural skills, the use of gardens as a specific vehicle to realize such intentions is nothing new.

Apart from history, historicism and the physical re-configuration of a landscape as a means to either engage with history or historically alter a terrain, design strategies such as collage and pastiche have also effectively served as tools to achieve the same goals. The depiction of fragments and the construction of 'isolated events' that draw on past associations use imagery as a means of rooting a work in the culture of a place.

The Mughal Garden at Rashtrapati Bhawan, for example, with its circular fountains of sixteen-tiered lotus leaves draws on the pivotal role that the lotus plant plays in Hinduism. The classically designed building too demonstrates the use of Indian motifs – most notably the *chhatri* or canopy, the indigenous *chhajja* or overhanging eaves and the *jaali* (latticed) screens – to create associative parallels with the indigenous architecture.

Replete with extensive plantations, the Mughal Garden is evergreen due to the numerous moulsri, *Putranjiva roxburgii*, cypress, *Thuja orientalis* and China orange trees. The moulsri trees adjoining the water channels are pruned to resemble mushrooms and flower during the dry months of May and June. While the walkways are flanked alternatively by cypresses and China oranges, both of which help further accentuate the axiality of the garden, symbolically the cypress represents death and the afterlife, while the China oranges, with their constantly changing appearance, are representative of renewal and the celebration of life. The *Putranjiva roxburgii* trees have spread themselves over two gazebos located on the western end of the garden, providing welcome shade from the harsh Delhi sun. Articulating the various intersections and points

Above: Viewed through a colonnade are the symmetric gardens inside Amber Fort. The red sandstone and white marble fort was built in 1592 and was the capital of the Kuchwaha Rajputs.

of termination of the axes, the coniferous *Thuja orientalis* is engulfed by the golden duranta.

Creepers and fragrant shrubs are planted along the walls of the garden. They include Raat ki Rani, *Bignonia venusta* (golden showers), *Rhyncospermum*, *Tecoma grandiflora* and the Rangoon creeper. With more than 250 varieties of roses, the gardens at the Presidential Estate represent some of the finest collections of roses to be found anywhere. Furthermore, various herbaceous annuals and biennials are grown. Planting of flowers takes place twice a year at these gardens and the numerous winter plants include gerbera, mesembryanthemum, brachycome, etc. Among the other winter plants that attract a number of visitors are dahlia, chrysanthemum, marigold, linum, etc.

The plantations are arranged within five distinctly marked zones of the garden. The main section is at the centre and flanked on the north and the south by two smaller terrace gardens, each surrounding a water tank. The flowers and trees planted here are the same as those in the larger central garden. These two gardens are commonly referred to as the Terrace Gardens because of their relative elevation. Connecting the circular Sunken or Butterfly Garden, which abounds in butterflies, is the Long or 'Purdah' Garden. Encased in walls that are twelve feet high, this garden has sixteen beds of roses encased in low hedges. A red sandstone pergola that runs the length of the garden over a ventral pavement is covered with rose creepers, bougainvillea, petrea and grape vines. The walls of this garden have China orange trees planted along them. At the culmination of this axis is the circular Rose Garden.

Located at the western extremity of the gardens, the Rose Garden with its central pond and fragrant varieties of plants such as stock (*Matthiola incana*), verbena (*Verbena officinalis*) and mignonette (*Reseda odorata*), is also home to one of the finest bonsai collections in the country.

Above: Entrance garden to the Samodh Palace.

Shiv Niwas Palace Hotel, Udaipur, with its numerous courts and upper level gardens, was originally the residence of Maharaja Fateh Singhji.

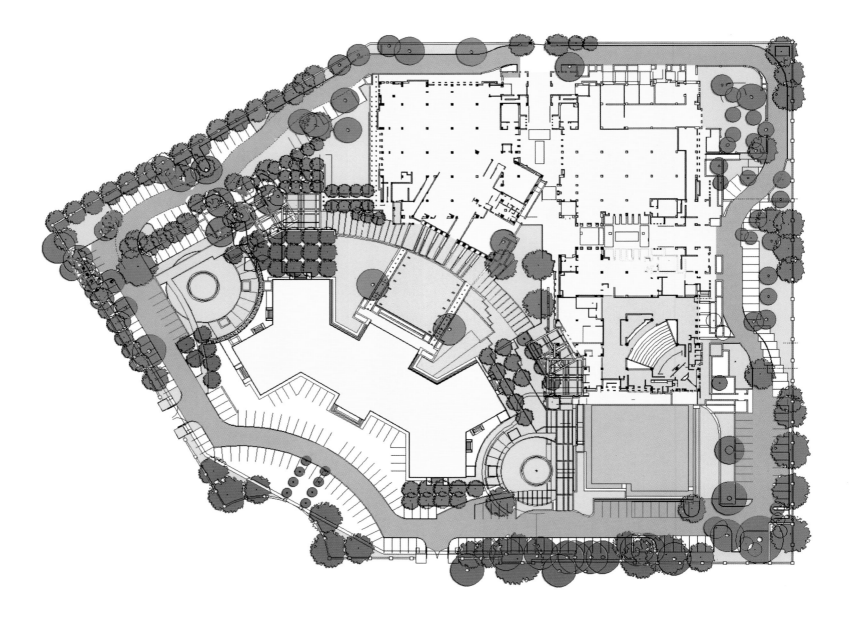

A short distance away, at the other end of Rajpath or Kingsway as it was formerly called, is the stately Jaipur House, now home to the National Gallery of Modern Art. The winners of an architectural competition held to expand the gallery, the architectural firm TEAM led by Snehanshu Mukherjee and A.R. Ramanathan were confronted with the challenge of uniting the existing gallery with the new wings of the much expanded museum. Skilful site planning coupled with the dexterous use of landscape ultimately served to establish a seamless relationship between the existing building and the new complex.

Dictated by stringent building codes and bylaws, the designers in recognition of the stability of the architectural composition of Jaipur House opted to situate their intervention as close to the plot lines as possible. Not only did this critical decision ensure the autonomy of the existing building, but more importantly created an interstitial space that would ultimately serve to establish an

effective rapport between the new complex and the existing galleries.

The three square blocks that comprise the new wing in conjunction with the old building according to Mukherjee relocates the main entrance to within the complex as opposed to its periphery. The two rotundas that previously housed innocuous air conditioning equipment and supplementary storage facilities to achieve the requisite floor area ratio (a ratio that determines the permissible area that one can construct on a given parcel of land) were demolished to be re-created in the form of a screen with a centrally located planter. Not only did the re-creation pay homage to the original composition but also served as a device to guide visitors to

Above: Plan of the newly expanded National Gallery of Modern Art, previously known as Jaipur House, New Delhi. The new addition is defined by the three square blocks in the rear and the newly created entrance courtyard.

the newly constructed courtyard. Furthermore, the placement of a screen wall that is aligned with the older building led to the definition of the orthogonal central courtyard. Prior to the expansion of the museum, trees planted in a similar formation served to create the same sense of spatial definition. The existing jamun, neem, mango and amaltas groves were further augmented with similar new plantations. Intended to break the rigidity of the new blocks, the light wells for illuminating the basements are capped with unstructured bougainvillea.

While the making and expansion of a national museum or art gallery is a task of immense cultural responsibility, endowed on one by the nation state, the design of residences have historically been precusors of things to come. They are fuelled as much by a visionary patron's desire to manifest an idea in built form, as by the need to give expression to his affluence, power and influence. Sensing an opportunity in East India Company's increasing power, Indian royalty sought to further ratify their position, first through trade with their European counterparts, and then through the design of new palaces with European styles.

With increased interaction and subsequent influence the Indian princely states began to imitate their European counterparts in their building projects. While by the end of the eighteenth century, for example, Neoclassicism was much in vogue, the governors of Bengal based the Aina Mahal of 1837 (Murshidabad) on the Government House in Kolkata.[7] And while the Nizam of Hyderabad feverishly espoused the Palladian style (the Falaknuma, acquired in 1897 is of classical composition), Jai Vilas or Victory Palace in Gwalior, built by the Scindias to mark the occasion of the

Above: This photograph of the Falaknuma Palace in Hyderabad taken during the early 1900s captures the influence of English garden design. The façade captured here is in the Palladian style while the rear of the building is in the Indo-Saracenic style.

Prince of Wales visit in 1858, further contributed to the stylistic development of Neoclassicism in India. Designed by Colonel Sir Michael Filose, this sprawling palace is arranged around a large court with the palace wings flanking its each side and was set in formal landscaped grounds.

Likewise, the majestic Umaid Bhawan palace set on twenty-six acres of land with fifteen acres of gardens was designed by H.V. Lanchester. Umaid Singh, a prominent Rajput who ruled from 1918 to 1947 embarked upon the construction of this art deco palace partly as a means to 'relieve distress caused by famine' and to create employment.[8] Unfortunately , the desert state of Rajasthan and Jodhpur in particular has always had scarcity of water, thereby making it ever the more challenging to maintain such lavish grounds.

However, it wasn't only the English who influenced the designs of princely residences in India. The French architect, M. Marcel for example, built for the ruling Sikh family of Kapurthala the equivalent of a French chateau in the plains of the Punjab, sited like the Palace of Versailles within a grandiose park complete with

an allegorical sanctuary. Located directly in front of the entrance is a circular marble fountain with figures and animals adorning it. Deers, panthers and other such animals carved in stone are also visible in the vicinity.[9]

While history and historicism are undoubtedly among the number of themes that provided the conceptual framework within which landscapes were conceived in India, the need for 'place-making', especially within the context of twentieth century modernism, came to the fore with many projects. The individual contribution of Nek Chand, a city road official in Le Corbusier's Chandigarh is most worthy of note.

Criticism grew against the overtly pragmatic approach of modernism and the characterless and banal landscapes that were, under the pretext of 'modern design', beginning to define public

Above: A sectional drawing cut through Nek Chand's rock garden in Chandigargh. The drawing illustrates the relationship between the landscape and his sculptures, some of which were cut into and embedded in the landscape

and private, urban and rural environments. The historical references and typological allusions that made gardens such as the Mughal Garden at Rashtrapati Bhawan praiseworthy, the romanticized and nostalgic notions of the past that they drew from did not befit Nehru's vision for a new and modern India. Furthermore, the use of historical references and type as a means to root a design within the greater cultural landscape of a place presupposed some level of homogeneity among the populace. Such a strategy was particularly apt for regimes that were either autocratic or dictatorial. With the advent of democracy and specifically, geographical and social mobility, it soon became untenable to communicate a design intent based on references that appealed only to a select few.

Thus modern architecture inevitably began to embrace a 'machine' analogy (Le Corbusier said that a house is a machine for living in) and professed the omnipotent 'grid' as the vehicle of choice in its manifestation of vastly homogenized landscapes. As a unifying tool that could spread itself endlessly and omni-directionally, much like a Mondrian painting, the grid was largely responsible for the banality of some of our landscapes.

Symbolic of man's position within the natural world, the taming of landscapes and the making of gardens articulates not only the specificity of a spatial experience but also brings the unique spirit of the place to the fore. The innate desire to 'make a place' motivated Nek Chand, a road inspector in Chandigarh, to build his now famous Rock Garden.

Having moved to the 'City Beautiful', as Chandigarh was referred to during 1947, the year of Partition, Nek Chand found forested land near Sukhna lake in the city that seemed to offer him an opportunity to express what he so eloquently describes as his 'belief that any conflict between nature's will and man's design is bound to lead to an overall destruction. The dimensions of the essential harmony between man and nature can be economic, social, political and aesthetic. My own effort is to explore the

Above: Nek Chand's Rock Garden in Chandigarh is the result of a single man's determined efforts. Made out of waste and recyclable material, the garden was built bit by bit over a period of eighteen years and was finally given legal sanction in 1976. A series of statues influenced by folk art are present throughout the twenty-five-acre park.

aesthetic dimension. The natural environment, trees, water, soil, birds, rocks are the major participants in my work'.

Working both diligently and surreptitiously in the evenings for over eighteen years, Nek Chand created a palette of materials that included pieces of broken crockery, fused fluorescent tube-lights, glass bangles, feathers, gravel, oil drums and waste material. The sculptural garden spread over twenty-five acres includes figures of animals, birds and human beings, its contribution towards the development of an aesthetic being a more profound form of folk art, espousing as it did the need to re-use, reduce and recycle.

Discovered in 1975 and noted as being an illegal construction on government land, the Rock Garden was threatened with demolition. Public opinion, however, swayed the authorities and in 1976, the garden was officially opened to the public, with Nek Chand given legal sanction to develop it further. Additional recognition of his contribution came with the Indian Post commemorating the garden, and by extension Nek Chand, in 1983 with a postage stamp.

'Place-making' does not fall solely within the purview of the individual architect or designer. For example, in his lecture while accepting the RAIA (Royal Australian Institute of Architects) Gold Medal, Kerry Hill, the architect of the ITC Sonar Bangla in Kolkata, stressed the role of historical precedent while simultaneously referring to 'the felt structure of reality', a notion that infuses a place with a uniqueness specific to its locale.

Addressing the audience he said, 'There is a need to find in architecture those abstractions that approach the essence – the "felt structure of reality". In this respect, working without the base of consistent cultural or locational conditions poses a unique set of architectural challenges, for if architecture is perceived as image only, in the context of regional response, it is very easy to fall into a state of mind in which tradition takes over from innovation, or worse, innovation denies tradition. The regeneration of traditional

Above: Mahatma Gandhi's *samadhi* in New Delhi with its eternal flame burning is modern India's most evocative funerary garden.

forms or literal variants of past models – no matter how well they are crafted – can only stagnate the operational idea of tradition and, at worst, debase both itself and the past in that it fails to address the concerns of contemporary architecture. Equally, an architecture that denies its past is at risk of being skin-deep: architecture that is at home everywhere and nowhere.

'More than any other art, architecture takes time to reach its ultimate form. Through affinity, we align ourselves with ideas to which we aspire. They are necessary points of reference that shape our thinking on the long journey of architecture, during which we are required to accept, reject, adjust and react to the diverse web of ideas that combine to influence our collective and individual design attitudes.'

Set in the midst of fifteen acres, the ITC Sonar Bangla, a hotel in the West Bengal city of Kolkata, comprises two high-rise blocks and one low-rise block, accommodating a total of 231 rooms. Unified by an immense lily pond, the water gardens of the hotel, with their floating palms, meditation pavilions and fountains, draw on historical precedent within a transformational

context through both strategies of abstraction and critical re-interpretation.

The filigrees of timber, the terracotta screens, and the stone cladding all contribute to the creation of a mnemonic device that through its gardens and the spatial disposition of the buildings resonates with the greater spatial psyche of the city. However, what distinguishes these gardens from those presented so far is that as water gardens they are meant to be seen, not inhabited. The act of only seeing, against the possibility of physical inhabitation as a means of delight and partaking the aesthetic pleasure, is in marked contrast to the more historicist approach Bill Bensley adopted in

Above: Shivaji Park, witness to numerous political rallies has a number of constituent institutions that fulfil many important social roles.

Following pages: The influence of a *char-bagh* composition is evident in this elegant garden at the Ram Bagh Palace in Jaipur. Symmetrical plantations coupled with well conceived lighting contribute towards the making of a scenographic set.

153

his landscape plan for the Oberoi Group of Hotels in the Raj Vilas property in Jaipur.

Spread over thirty-two acres, the gardens of this boutique hotel are inspired, like those at Rashtrapati Bhawan, by those of the Mughal tradition. Manicured lawns punctuated with moats, fountains and lotus ponds in conjunction with a choreographed sequence of overlapping indoor and outdoor spaces all contribute to make the gardens part of a scenographic landscape. Pavilions interspaced within the landscape act as follies from which the viewer can absorb the hotel's architecture.

An elaborate network of sandstone paths and deep blue hand-made Jaipur tiles interconnect the estate. The 250-year-old Shiva temple, the gemstone of the grounds, is set in the midst of a lotus garden while the spa and health club, located to the west of it in a courtyard mansion, is flanked by a traditional herb garden and an extensive lotus pond.

While both gardens draw on historical precedent, the former uses the extensive water garden to unite the various elements of the scheme while the latter in its use of scenography, choreographs movement. Such choreography is an intrinsic part of homage where a visitor circumambulates, for example, a tomb in deference or respect for a past leader.

Marking the spot where he was cremated on 31 January 1948, Raj Ghat, the memorial of Mahatma Gandhi, consists of a raised black marble platform with his last words, 'Hey Ram' inscribed on it. Sydney Percy Lancaster, the secretary of the Agri-Horticultural Society of India and the last Englishman to hold the post of

Above: Spread over twenty acres, the Garden of Five Senses promises sensory pleasures, educational facilities, and spaces such as amphitheatres for public performances. Seen here are the pathways that interconnect the various components of this garden.

Facing page: The potent symbolism and iconography associated with the lotus continues to be a great source of inspiration for many Indian landscape designers. Seen here is a lotus pond in the Garden of Five Senses in New Delhi.

Tucked away behind ramparts and high walls, the relatively modern gardens of the Neemrana Fort Hotel serve to complement the architecture of this former fortification.

superintendent of horticultural operations, Government of India, did the landscaping and planting. The memorial was designed by Vanu Bhuta with an eternal flame burning perpetually at one end. Museums dedicated to Mahatma Gandhi adjoin the *samadhi* or memorial spot. Visitors and dignitaries traverse a stone footpath that leads them through earth bermes (mound of earth) to the walled enclosure of the funerary garden.

Visiting dignitaries, paying their respect to the 'Father of the Nation', lay large bouquets and wreaths at the memorial. The planting of a sapling by visitors of state has come to symbolically mark friendship, cooperation and mutual respect between two nations.

Gardens and constructed landscapes have historically been used as the venues from where political gatherings are addressed. At times the parks themselves have become synonymous with political change.

Notably, Shivaji Park in the Dadar district of Mumbai, covering almost two square kilometres is an area that has witnessed numerous such political gatherings. Lal Bahadur Shastri, for example, the

then prime minister of India, addressed a *vijay sabha* or victory gathering at the end of the 1965 war against Pakistan. More recently, the Shiv Sena uses the park extensively for its political rallies. The park, however, was built in 1925 by the Bombay Municipal Corporation. Named after the Maratha ruler and warrior Chhatrapati Shivaji, the park consists of many institutions which play important social roles.

In contrast (because it is used for leisure, this park houses a zoo and has the museum gardens) is the Rani Jijamata Udyaan (formerly known as the Victoria Gardens) in the Byculla district of central Mumbai, which houses the city zoo and the Victoria and Albert Museum. Established in 1861 and set within forty-eight acres, the Udyaan features a clock tower and one of the city's best kept botanical gardens as well.

Above: The residential courtyard continues to be used as a public space or an 'open air living room' within the larger confines of a home. Deep-set verandahs and adjoining rooms open on to it and are often used as the main circulation route within the house.

Constructed just twenty years apart, in 1881, the Hanging Gardens or Ferozeshah Mehta Gardens on Mumbai's Malabar Hill is a haven for the city's elite. Offering splendid views of the Arabian Sea, the garden with its numerous sculpted hedges provides visual relief in an otherwise densely populated part of the city. Unlike Shivaji Park, which is associated with political activism, the Hanging Gardens are believed to have been built over a reservoir to protect the water from the contaminating activities of the nearby Towers of Silence – a funerary raised circular structure, where the Parsis expose their dead.

Named the Garden City, Bengaluru houses the famous garden, Lal Bagh. Commissioned by Hyder Ali in 1760 and finished by his son Tipu Sultan, it is home to over a thousand species of flora. With trees over a hundred years old and a large collection of rare plants, along with ancient rock formations, the garden at Lal Bagh, along with its reputed 3,000-million-year-old rock formations, is a huge draw for visitors. Patterned in part on the Mughal gardens in Sira (the southernmost Mughal province, which is approximately 120 kilometres away), the 240-acre garden features the Glass House,

built in a design influenced by Joseph Paxton's glass and cast-iron Glass Crystal Palace in London's Hyde Park. Built for the Great Exhibition of 1851, the Crystal Palace was built to showcase the new materials and constructional technologies that the Industrial Revolution had brought with it, the Glass House in Bengaluru communicating the same ideals.

While conventional categorization may not be followed to describe large parks built towards the end of the nineteenth and early twentieth century as part of the modern Indian landscape, their development did coincide with the birth of democracy in the subcontinent and like Shivaji Park, they were used for political activism. The construction of the Glass House by John Cameron, the Lal Bagh's superintendent in the 1870s does in fact exemplify another one of the key traits of modernism, the use of 'new' industrialized materials of construction.

Above: A well, with its tiled pitched roof, serves as a focal point for part of the garden and the bordering manicured lawns.

Not to be overshadowed by Lal Bagh, Cubbons Park, stretching over 250 acres, is equally large. Officially known as Sri Chamarajendra Park, it was established in 1870 by John Meade, the then acting commissioner of Mysore, with Major General Richard Sankey, chief engineer of the state who conceived the landscape designs. Originally called Meade Park and then Cubbon Park, it was renamed in 1927 as Sri Chamarajendra Park to commemorate the silver jubilee of Sri Krishnaraja Wodeyar's rule in Mysore.

The park, originally designed over an area of one hundred acres, has expanded considerably over the years. Among the indigenous species that can be seen are artocarpus, amaltas (*Cassia fistula*), and ficus, while the more exotic species include bamboo, *Grevillea robusta* (amongst the first silver oaks to be planted in Bengaluru after being imported from Australia), and *Swietenia mahagoni*. A number of statues, most notably those of Queen Victoria, King Edward VII, Major General Sir Mark Cubbon, who served as the commissioner of Mysore from 1834 to 1861, Rajya

Dhurandhara, Sir K. Sheshadri Iyer and Sri Chamarajendra Wodeyar are spread across the park.

While over the years the nature of patronage has shifted, the imperatives for the making of and subsequent dedication of parks and gardens have changed little. For example, Buddha Jayanti Park in New Delhi was built to commemorate the 2,500th anniversary of Lord Gautama Buddha's attainment of nirvana. A sapling from the Bodhi tree in Sri Lanka, whose lineage can be traced back to the parent tree in Bodh Gaya under which Lord Buddha attained

Above: The reflecting pool in the foreground captures the image of the North and South Secretariat Blocks designed by Sir Herbert Baker. Water, whether in the form of fountains or pools has historically played an integral role in the constructed landscapes of the Indian subcontinent.

Facing page: An aerial view down Rajpath or Kingsway, as it was previously called. Rashtrapati Bhawan can be seen in the background while India Gate defines the other end of this ceremonial axis. Flanking it on either side are lawns and pools.

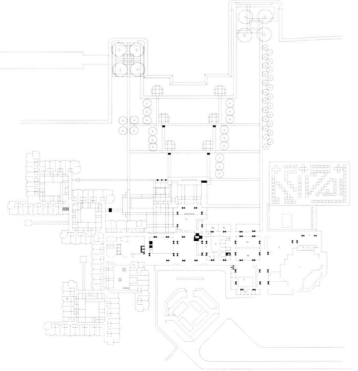

enlightenment, has been planted here. The park was dedicated in October 1993 by the fourteenth Dalai Lama and is used as a venue for a variety of programmes and discussions by the different Buddhist sects and organizations in the city.

While religion has long been a motivating factor in the creation of sacred groves and temple gardens, and as is evident continues till today, the design of gardens for sheer sensory pleasure is also a strong tradition that continues. Commissioned by the Delhi Tourism and Transportation Development Corporation, the Garden

Above: Set against the backdrop of the Himalayan range, the stepped terraces and water channels of Shalimar Gardens in Srinagar were once accessed directly from the adjoining Dal lake before the construction of a neighbouring road.

Left: Plan of the Kashmir Convention Centre and its adjoining gardens. The gardens at once align themselves with and distance themselves from the neighbouring historic gardens of Shalimar and Nishat Bagh.

of Five Senses in New Delhi's Said-ul-Ajaib village near Mehrauli, was inaugurated in 2003.

Conceived as a garden that would actively engage and heighten the sensory perception of visitors, these gardens, unlike those that use symbolism as the predominant vehicle of communication, subscribe to a phenomenological frame of thought. These gardens comprise a number of parts, most notably, the 'colour gardens' that have flowering shrubs and ground cover laid in a variety of compositions. The 'courts of specimen' plants showcase rare species like the cactii, teak, and Arjun and camphor herbs, among others, while the Khas Bagh along the spiral walkway is composed like a formal Mughal garden. Visitors are encouraged to engage directly with the plants and other natural elements through their senses of sight, smell and touch as the gardens were conceived and designed specifically from that perspective.

The centrally located Lodhi Garden, also in New Delhi, is home to the tombs of both the Lodhi and the Sayyid rulers. With the highly visible tomb of Mohammed Shah, the third ruler of the Sayyid dynasty (1434-44), adjoining the main road along with the further inset monuments such as the tomb of Sikander Lodhi, the Bara Gumbad (Large Dome), the Sheesh Gumbad, a three-domed mosque, the remains of a courtyard residence and a mosque, the gardens were for the better part home to squatters until the British evicted them in the nineteenth century. Lady Willingdon, after whom the grounds were named intermittently, was instrumental in the landscaping of the lawns at the time. However, it was not until 1968 that Joseph Allen Stein and Garrett Eckbo re-designed the gardens to give it its present form. In the 1970s, a bonsai garden was added on the eastern corner as was a greenhouse, also designed by Stein. With trees and plants such as chir, deodar, chinar, neem and eucalyptus, the garden has over the years become a favourite with residents of the city.

Above: Dal lake transforms itself into a water garden with lotuses engulfing the lone *shikara-wala* (boatsman) and houseboat.

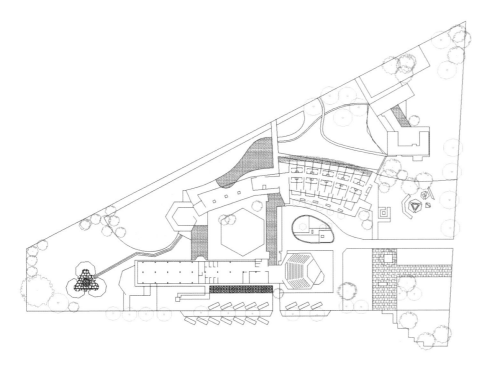

Adjoining the historic tombs is the India International Centre (1962) and the greater Lodhi Estate where Stein went on to build buildings such as the Ford Foundation Headquarters (1968), the Council for Scientific and Industrial Research (1970), the Green House at Lodhi Garden (1971), the headquarters for UNICEF (1981), and the World Wild Life Fund for Nature – India (1989). With regard to the choice of site for the India International Centre, Stein had said:

> The proximity of the beautiful Lodhi Gardens influenced the choice of this location for the India International Centre. A particularly fortunate aspect of the Lodhi Gardens site is the soft quality of light . . . a wonderfully refreshing change from the harsh, dust-laden atmosphere of the Delhi summer. The park's many fine vistas are notable for a charming alternation of soft green light and long shadows across the shrub-studded lawns . . . culminating dramatically at the

Above: Plan of the India International Centre that was designed by Joseph A. Stein.

Right: An aerial view of the India International Centre taken from Lodhi Garden. Seen in the foreground are the amphitheatre, the pond, and the manicured lawns. The building and the landscape both share a symbiotic relationship.

166

various monumental tombs with their rugged stone walls and strongly proportioned domes.[10]

Recognizing both the potency of the site and the delicacy of the environment, Stein 'designed the Centre with the objective that it be an appropriate modern addition to the garden landscape, expressing the techniques and more informal attitudes of the twentieth century. Its siting and development is based on a varying sequence of indoor spaces and outdoor courtyard spaces, rather than on the commanding axial relationships employed in the designs of Lutyens, Baker and the Mughal architects'.[11]

The recognition and subsequent articulation of the intent to create a building that is an extension of the landscape, along with the rejection of the formality of the Mughal garden type, was unprecedented within the greater landscape of modern India. By

not constructing anything on the ground level other than a long open verandah flanked by walls only on its width served to not only open up the courtyard, but also to embrace the dense foliage of the adjoining Lodhi Garden. Skilfully done, Stein managed to invoke both a sense of closure, something a courtyard by definition should have, and a choreographed openness that constantly engages and teases the mind. The virtuosity exhibited in the manipulation of both scale and proportion is amply evident in the manner in which the varied elements of the landscape, trees, ponds and lawns, along with the functional requirements of the building, are integrated to allow each to assert an individuality of its own while contributing to a collective, harmonious composition.

The contribution made by this ensemble of buildings and landscape towards the creation of a modern Indian idiom cannot be

underestimated or undermined. At once rejecting the precedent representatives of bygone eras, their symbols and their myths, Stein's Lodhi Estate established a link between both the natural and built environment, modernity and history, and perhaps most importantly, along with a handful of architects like Le Corbusier and Louis Kahn, freed the newly formed Indian state from the shackles of a potentially overbearing history by demonstrating the ways in which one could strike a symbiotic relationship between the two.

Completed in 1984, also by Stein, the Kashmir Conference Centre was conceived by Stein as 'a celebration of nature'. Writing at the time of laying the foundation stone in 1977 he said, 'The effort has been to create buildings and gardens that would merge into the surroundings, add focus upon a lovely scene, and in the process bring sympathetic attention to this gravely threatened place of natural beauty. Accordingly the design integrates building, garden and lake into an entity so that the visitor should be able to experience the special mode of nature that makes a visit to Kashmir so memorable.' [12]

The Conference Centre, located on the picturesque Dal lake, is in close proximity to such historic gardens as Shalimar Bagh and Nishat Bagh. With the mountains rising up on the north and the lake lying beyond it, the site for the Conference Centre and its gardens is both delicate and demanding.

Above: The swimming pool of the Oberoi Amarvilas Hotel in Agra, accessed through a series of stepped terraces, is bound on one side by a pavilion-like structure reminiscent of traditional Mughal architecture.

The decision to locate the building near the water's edge was critical from a number of perspectives. Foremost among them would have been the reduced perceptible height of the complex as it now stands on the lowest part of the mountain. Furthermore, by being adjacent to the water's edge, it allows access by *shikara* (water taxi) as well. Stein had intended the building to serve as both a gateway and focal point for a proposed nature reserve and recreational park that was to be sited north of the complex and its location would certainly have aided this.

Much like its historic neighbours, the gardens at the Conference Centre step down the landscape towards the lake. Pedestrian pathways are flanked by magnolia trees that along with their adjoining paths are successively offset as they approach the water. The paths terminate either in fountains or in a flight of steps. At the water's edge, the gardens embrace the lake by allowing it to penetrate the garden. Like at the India International Centre, the gardens at the Conference Centre do not adhere to the strict symmetrical relationships that are characteristic of the *char-bagh*, but instead respond directly to the specificities of the site.[13]

Working decades later and at the scale of a residence in Kolkata's Alipore neighbourhood, the architect Abhimanyu Dalal, along with the landscape architect Savita Punde, exploited the distinction between the two senses of sight and touch in their design of the Nopanys' residence. Presenting a hard and stoic northern exterior, the house and the garden together constitute a constructed landscape within a greater urban situation. The extensive use of large sheets of plate glass, coupled with a climatic-controlled interior space, allowed the architects to create a perceptual disjunction in which what you see is not how you feel.

A view of the Nopany residence from the gardens. The extensive use of large sheets of glass along with wooden cladding and accompanying *brise soleils* (sun breakers) re-interpret historic pavilions and integrate them with the rest of the house. Pools and decorative walls within the landscape are interspersed with each other in the entire composition.

The main living space located towards the south of the house encompasses within it a highly sophisticated manipulation of the section. This coupled with the perceptual shift creates a spatial environment that is evocative, simultaneously in parts, of a shaded garden pavilion, and of an outdoor room.

With the geometrical plan of the house reflected selectively in the garden and the judicious but deliberate use of materials that draw the landscape deep within the house just as it projects itself outwards, this residence distinguishes itself from earlier precedents in two distinct ways. The first is the recognition and amalgamation of established garden and architectural typologies. Evident here are attributes of the walled garden in as much as we can see the perceptual 'openness' of garden pavilions. The second is a complementary vocabulary between the stark white planes of the façade, its accompanying wooden louvres and glass and stone cladding with such landscape elements as the pool (which falls

within the greater envelope of the house), the reflecting pool, plantations and sculptural figures that serve to extend the perceptual experience of the main living room.

Adopting a strategy distinct from that of the Nopany house, the design of the Bahá'í temple, in New Delhi breaks new ground in the manner in which it abstracts the imagery associated with a traditional Indian plant.

Set amidst twenty-six acres of land and completed in December 1986, the temple of the Bahá'í faith in New Delhi continues the tradition of architectural splendour. The architect, Fariborz Sahba,

Above: With dense plantations surrounding it, a reflecting pool frames a part of the house.

Facing page: Views from within the house display elements such as plantations in the gardens, drawing one's eye out towards the landscape and thereby extending one's spatial perception.

after travelling extensively in India and studying religious architecture and iconography, chose to model the temple after a half-open lotus flower. Viewed from the outside, the lotus has three sets of leaves or petals. Each of these elements is repeated nine times. The concrete shells that constitute them are clad in marble quarried from the Mount Pentilekon mines in Greece. The marble was then sent to Italy for cutting before being installed on the site. The first row, or 'entrance leaves', opens outwards and defines the nine entrances around the hall. The next set of nine petals, or 'outer leaves', points inwards and in conjunction with the 'entrance leaves' encloses the outer hall. The third set, or the 'inner leaves', is partly closed, forming the main structure housing the central hall of the temple.

The elegance of the whole structure conceals the complexity that lay in its construction. The shell surfaces on both sides of the ridge of the entrance, and the 'outer leaves', for example, are formed from spheres of varying radii whose centres lie at different points within the building. In addition, the two surfaces of the shells of the 'entrance leaves' also belong to spheres of different radii. Plotting the complex geometry on the construction site in a manner that could be easily communicable to a foreman and site engineer was in itself a feat.

While the nine pools that surround the temple represent the floating leaves of a lotus plant, the water also helps to ventilate the building. Given the harsh summer heat of Delhi and its varying degrees of humidity, the architect, in lieu of sophisticated and expensive air conditioning systems, modelled the ventilation system on ancient and effective technologies.

Based on a series of smoke tests conducted at the Imperial College, London, on a model of the temple, cool air is drawn up through the basement after having passed over the pools, as hot air

Designed by the Canadian architect Fariborz Sahba, the temple of the Bahá'í faith is modelled on a lotus flower. The 'white petals' that enclose the spaces below are arranged in three concentric rings. Made of concrete and clad in marble the 'lotus' leaves take on sculptural proportions.

175

The integration of ponds, pathways and gardens with the temple structure, along with the imagery associated with a lotus flower, is captured in this unusual aerial photograph of the Bahá'í Temple in New Delhi.

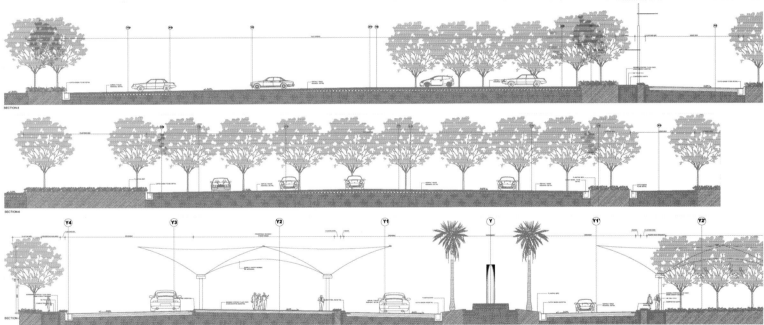

Above: An architectural section drawing cut through the key landscapes of the newly renovated Chhatrapati Shivaji International Airport (Mumbai) illustrates the relationship between vehicular traffic, pedestrian routes, landscape elements, plantations and the accompanying tensile structures.

Top: Seemlessly integrating complex vehicular and pedestrian circulation patterns, the new design, with its tent-like tensile structures, colourful plantations and water features, defines the airport's visual identity.

Facing page: The creation of a 'civic space' as defined in part by the tent-like structures has aided the transformation of the airport from a mere transportation hub to a social space of collective civic identity.

Following pages: The central communal space at the Embassy Golf Links Business Park (EGLBP) in Bengaluru is defined as much by the variety of landscape elements present – fountains, ponds, pergolas, pavings and plantations – as by the architecture that encloses it.

The upper level podium landscape of the Kalpataru Horizon residences in Worli, Mumbai, with its sinuously curved pathways and geometrically ordered plantation beds, guides visitors around the buildings. This upper level garden astutely allowed for the creation of parking spaces at the ground level.

leaves the building through the dome. A set of exhaust fans in the dome cools the concrete shells to reduce heat transfer while another set pushes the air from the auditorium into the basement and then back into the auditorium after having been cooled. The natural ventilation stack uses the pools in the landscape along with the geometry of the temple to ensure an effective and environment-friendly cooling solution.

When interviewed about the choice of the iconography employed for the building, the architect said, 'I was looking for a concept that would be acceptable to the people of all the different religions that abound with such rich diversity in India. I wanted to design something new and unique, at the same time not strange but familiar, like the Bahá'í faith itself, something which would be loved by the people of different religions. It should, on the one hand, reveal the simplicity, clarity and freshness of the Bahá'í Revelation, as apart from the beliefs and man-made concepts of the many divided sects. On the other hand, it should show respect for the basic beliefs of all the religions of the past and act as a constant reminder to the followers of each faith that the principles of all the religions of God are one. People should intuitively find some sort of relationship with it in their hearts . . . the lotus represents the Manifestation of God, and is also a symbol of purity and tenderness. Its significance is deeply rooted in the minds and hearts of the Indians. In the epic poem *Mahabharata*, the Creator Brahma is described as having sprung from the lotus that grew out of Lord Vishnu's navel when that deity lay absorbed in meditation. There is a deep and universal reverence for the lotus, which is regarded as a sacred flower associated with worship throughout many centuries. In Buddhist folklore the Boddhisatva Avalokiteswara is represented as born from a lotus, and is usually depicted as standing or sitting on a lotus pedestal and holding a lotus bloom in his hand. Buddhists glorify him in their prayers, "Om Mani Padme Hum" (Yea, O Jewel in the Lotus). Lord Buddha says you have to be like a lotus which,

Above: A water screen at the Kalpataru gardens frames the view of a lone tree in a box planter.

Varied plantations capture and define pathways between lanscape elements in the gardens of the Kalpataru Horizon project in Mumbai.

Left: A night view of the podium gardens at the Kalpataru Horizon, Mumbai, reveals the complementary relationship between the buildings and the landscape.

although living in dirty water, still remains beautiful and undefiled by its surroundings.

'So, we realize that the lotus is associated with worship, and has been a part of the life and thoughts of Indians through the ages. It will seem to them as though they have been worshipping in this Temple in their dreams for years. Now their vision has become a reality and, God willing, some day they will all enter and worship in it.'

Other landscape projects done by Design Cell (Ravi and Savita Punde) are the residential complex Kalpataru Horizon in Mumbai, the Chhatrapati Shivaji International Airport (CSIA) frontage and the fifty-acre Embassy Golf Links Business Park in Bengaluru.

The twin thirty-storey towers of the Kalpataru Horizon residential complex are set on three acres of land and rise from a large podium raised on columns around which, at the ground level, are parking spaces. As an upper level or terrace garden at an enormous scale, it has undesirable urban views 'screened out' by a five-meter-high wall. Punctured at select points to allow the eye to travel, the wall acts both as screen and scenographic pointer. Along the west however, the openings in the wall are larger so as to allow

in the sea breeze. Elements such as seating niches, pergolas and in-built pockets for plantations characterize various parts of the wall.

Sinuous curves reflecting the towers along with the straight lines of the structural grids inform the language of the landscape. Linear bands of ground cover (plantations) lead the eye to articulated pockets while the curved paths are reinforced visually by the adjoining pebble drain. An amphitheatre nestles in one corner, while a custom-designed kid's zone is located within the stilt area so as to provide an all-weather facility. Additionally, each tower is equipped with a rooftop swimming pool.

The Chhatrapati Shivaji International Airport (CSIA) in Mumbai differs considerably from the Kalpataru project. As a work that is part urban infrastructure, part landscape, two key concerns

Above: The abstracted and sculptural fountains at the Embassy Golf Links Business Park (EGLBP) in Bengaluru.

Facing page: An aerial view looking down at the stepped terraces that bind the perimeter of the Embassy Golf Links Business Park (EGLBP) in Bengaluru.

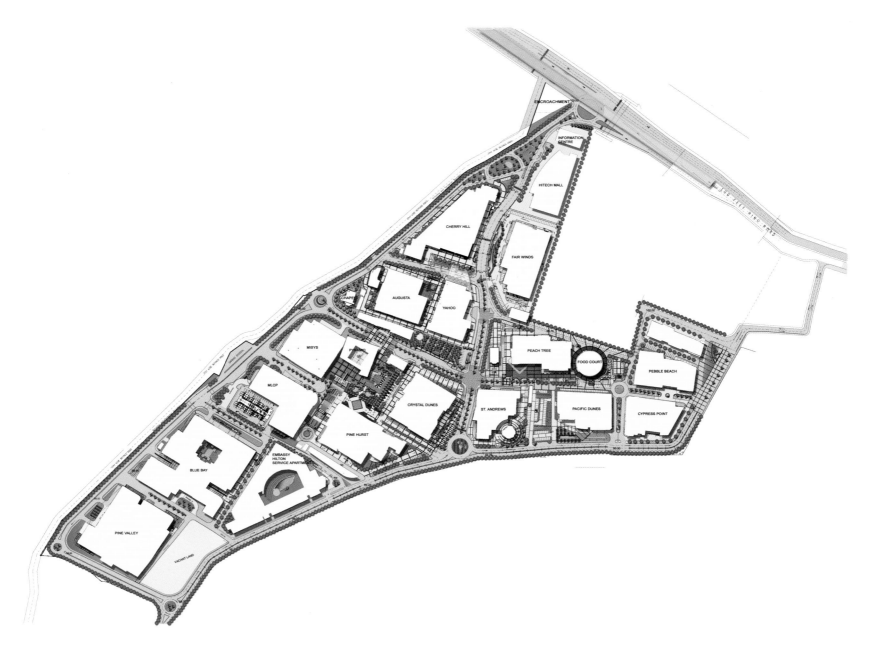

of the project were the need to ensure that passengers could reach their mode of local transport under roof cover (the torrential monsoon rains made this a necessity) and the desire to create a civic space that Mumbaikars could be proud of.

In consultation with the traffic and transportation planner, a detailed circulation plan at the terminals determining areas of parking, passenger pickup and drop-off, the segregation of vehicular categories such as taxis, three-wheeler auto richshaws, and private vehicles along with special categories for the physically handicapped and VIPs were addressed in the design. Pedestrian thoroughfare was made as raised pavements across the roads. However, this done, the desire to transcend the airport from being a mere response to a given set of circulation criteria and to create a civic space that would define the airport complex, led to the introduction of a central plaza. As a multi-functional public space, this was to include information kiosks, food courts, and a space for placard holders.

Water bodies and planter beds contributed towards creating an amiable ambience while simultaneously serving as physical barriers. Extended arms for pickup of passengers aided in reducing congestion and assuring availability of ample room in its forecourt. Tensile canopies spanned to cover the bays and when backlit, their illumination created a dramatic entrance to the terminals.

The fifty-acre Embassy Golf Links Business Park in Bengaluru is a multi-tenanted software campus wherein the landscape unifies and organizes the external circulation routes between the buildings. Plazas and amphitheatres were developed as exterior congregation spaces while a wi-fi zone or cyber trail interconnects two food courts. Furthermore, a pedestrian spine was developed as a leisure zone with information kiosks, seating, planter beds and pavilions.

Water features and planting were developed to homogenize the

Above: A site plan of the Embassy Golf Links Business Park, Bengaluru.

open space development while the geometry of the landscape was based on the architectural lines of the campus. Ground cover beds and low planters, along with water pools and spill edges were extensively used while columnar date palms broke the sightlines. The earth forms in the design are intended to mirror the undulating fairways of the adjoining KGA golf course.

The extension of and creation of perceptual realities do in many ways form the cornerstone of the intricate landscapes that constitute the gardens of India. The primordial relationship between a people and their land has led to the development of gardens that exist not only in the physical realm but also play a key role in the formation of an identity of a people. Whether through early textual references, the depiction of paradise in carpets or the enactment of the social order in palace and funerary gardens, the role played by plants, gardens, constructed and natural landscapes in the Indian subcontinent cannot be underestimated. The symbolism associated

with plants such as the lotus is so deeply engraved in the Indian psyche that Lutyens chose to model fountains at the Presidential Palace on it. Likewise, the extensive water and lotus garden at the recently completed Sonar Bangla in Kolkata further reiterates the potency and deep-rooted cultural affinity for such ancient forms that necessitates their contemporary re-invention.

Undoubtedly, given the longevity and inherent complexity of the greater Indian civilization, the 'gardens' that history has allowed to endure serve as important cultural markers. As works that we both reside in and enact the practice of everyday living in, as well as those we use to commemorate, the gardens of India have played a definitive role in the expression of the will of a people and the making of an enduring physical and cultural landscape.

Above: Boxed plantations interspersed with water channels and palm trees create an axis at the Embassy Golf Links Business Park in Bengaluru.

ENDNOTES

GARDENS REMEMBERED

1. Priyaleen Singh, "Vatikas of Lore" in 'Enchanted Gardens', *The Hindu* – folio, *Sunday Magazine* (4 June 2000), http://www.hinduonnet.com/folio/fo0006/00060160.htm
2. Ibid.
3. 'Gardening in Ancient India', http://society.indianetzone.com/Gardening/1/gardening_ancient_india.htm
4. References and facts for the preceding text were collated from a number of sources, most notably, 'Gardening in Ancient India' as in the previous note.
5. S. Ananth, *The Penguin Guide to Vastu: The Classical Indian Science of Architecture and Design* (New Delhi Viking, 1998); also, *Wikipedia*, http://en.wikipedia.org/wiki/Vastu_Shastra
6. R. Thapar, *Ashoka and the Decline of the Mauryas* (London: Oxford University Press, 1961).
7. Partha Mitter, 'Indian Art' in *Oxford History of Art* (New Delhi: Oxford University Press, 2001), pp.13-15.
8. L. Feer, ed., *Samyutta Nikaya*, 6 vols. (London: Pali Text Society, 1884-1904); translated as *The Book of Kindred Sayings* (London: Pali Text Society, 1917-1930), C.A.F. Rhys Davids and F.L. Woodward, trans., part 3, 128.
9. Partha Mitter, 'Indian Art' in *Oxford History of Art* (New Delhi: Oxford University Press, 2001), p.15.
10. Ibid.
11. Kate Nesbitt, *Theorizing a New Agenda for Architecture: An Anthology of Architectural Theory* (Princeton: Princeton Architectural Press, 1965-1995, paperback, 1996), pp. 74-76.
12. George Michell and Antonio Marinelli, *The Royal Palaces of India* (London: Thames and Hudson, 2004), p. 10.
13. Ibid., p. 68.

MY GARDEN, MY PARADISE

1. Kate Nesbitt, *Theorizing a New Agenda for Architecture: An Anthology of Architectural Theory* (Princeton: Princeton Architectural Press, 1965-1995, paperback, 1996), p. 44.
2. Typological categorization for gardens from 'Garden and Designed Landscape Types', http://www.gardenvisit.com/history_theory/garden_landscape_design_articles/garden_types/garden_types
3. *Wikipedia*, http://en.wikipedia.org/wiki/Kaziranga
4. Naditha Krishna, "Retreat of the Gods" in 'Enchanted Gardens', *The Hindu* – folio, *Sunday Magazine* (4 June 2000), http://www.hinduonnet.com/folio/fo0006/00060180.htm
5. Ibid.
6. 'Indian Botanic Garden, Howrah', *Botanical Survey of India,* http://164.100.52.111/indianBotanicgarden.shtm

OF TEMPLES, PALACES AND TOMBS

1. Christopher Tadgell, *The History of Architecture in India: From the Dawn of Civilization to the End of the Raj* (London: Phaidon, 1990), pp.149-151.
2. C.M. Stuart Villiers, *Gardens of the Great Mughals* (New Delhi: Asian Educational Services, 2007), p.16.
3. Catherine B. Asher, *Architecture of Mughal India* (Cambridge: Cambridge University Press, 1992), p. 20.
4. C.M. Stuart Villiers, *Gardens of the Great Mughals* (New Delhi: Asian Educational Services, 2007), pp. 38-40.
5. Ibid.
6. *Wikipedia*, http://en.wikipedia.org/wiki/Din-i-Ilahi
7. Catherine B. Asher, *Architecture of Mughal India* (Cambridge: Cambridge University Press, 1992), p. 106.
8. D. Fairchild Ruggles, 'Humayun's Tomb and Garden: Typologies and Visual Order', in *Gardens in the Time of the Great Muslim Empires: Theory and Design*, ed., Attilio Petruccioli (Leiden; New York: E.J. Brill, 1997), p. 173.
9. Ibid., p. 174.
10. Ebba Koch, *Mughal Architecture* (Munich: Prestel-Verlag, 1991), p. 46.
11. D. Fairchild Ruggles, 'Humayun's Tomb and Garden: Typologies and Visual Order', in *Gardens in the Time of the Great Muslim Empires: Theory and Design*, ed., Attilio Petruccioli (Leiden; New York: E.J. Brill, 1997), p. 174.
12. Glenn D. Lowry, 'Humayun's Tomb: Form, Function, and Meaning in Early Mughal Architecture', in *Muqarnas IV: An Annual on*

Islamic Art and Architecture, ed., Oleg Grabar (Leiden: E.J. Brill, 1987), pp. 133-148.

13. D. Fairchild Ruggles, 'Humayun's Tomb and Garden: Typologies and Visual Order', in *Gardens in the Time of the Great Muslim Empires: Theory and Design*, ed., Attilio Petruccioli (Leiden; New York: E.J. Brill, 1997), p. 177.

14. Lisa Golombek, *The Timurid Shrine at Gazur Gah* (Toronto: Royal Ontario Museum, 1969), pp. 102-103.

15. François Bernier, *Travels in the Mogul Empire: AD 1656-1668*, trans., Irving Brock, ann., Archibald Constable (1891); second ed. revised by Vincent A. Smith (1916; reprinted in New Delhi: Oriental Books Reprint Corporation, 1983), p. 298.

16. D. Fairchild Ruggles, 'Humayun's Tomb and Garden: Typologies and Visual Order', in Gardens in the Time of the Great Muslim Empires: *Theory and Design*, ed., Attilio Petruccioli (Leiden; New York: E.J. Brill, 1997), pp. 177-78.

17. C.M. Stuart Villiers, *Gardens of the Great Mughals* (New Delhi: Asian Educational Services, 2007), p. 109.

18. M. Abdullah Chaghtai, 'A Family of Great Mughal Architects', in *Islamic Culture*, XI, (April 1937), pp. 200-209.

19. Catherine B. Asher, *Architecture of Mughal India* (Cambridge: Cambridge University Press, 1992), p.212.

20. Priyaleen Singh, 'From Paradise to Picturesque: Changing Design Vocabularies of Mughal Gardens', http://www.nara.accu.or.jp/english/about/conference/pdf/02_p.pdf, p. 42.

21. Ibid., p. 44.

22. C.M. Stuart Villiers, *Gardens of the Great Mughals* (New Delhi: Asian Educational Services, 2007), p. 215.

23. Ibid., pp. 203-204.

24. Ibid., p. 109.

MODERN INDIA, MODERN LANDSCAPES

1. Robert Grant Irving, Indian Summer: *Lutyens, Baker and Imperial Delhi* (Yale: Yale University Press, 1984), p. 218.

2. Ibid., p. 223.

3. Ibid., p. 215.

4. Ibid., p. 226.

5. Deyan Sudjic, *The Edifice Complex: How the Rich and Powerful Shape the World* (New York: The Penguin Press, 2005), p. 12.

6. *Wikipedia*, http://en.wikipedia.org/wiki/Gardens_of_Versailles#The_Problem_of_Water

7. George Michell and Antonio Marinelli, *The Royal Palaces of India* (London: Thames and Hudson, 2004), p. 217.

8. Ibid., p. 222.

9. Ibid., p. 222.

10. Stein, unpublished project description for the India International Centre, New Delhi, 1959.

11. Stephen White, *Building in the Garden: The Architecture of Joseph Allen Stein in India and California* (New Delhi: Oxford University Press, 1993), p. 111.

12. Stein, in 'Kashmir Conference Centre', a brochure released for the foundation stone laying ceremony, Department of Public Works, Government of Jammu and Kashmir, India, 1977.

13. Stephen White, *Building in the Garden: The Architecture of Joseph Allen Stein in India and California* (New Delhi: Oxford University Press, 1993), pp. 275-277.

VISION OF PARADISE

1. Asha Rani Mathur, *Indian Carpets, A Hand Knotted Heritage* (New Delhi: Rupa & Co), pp. 7-15.

A BRIEF HISTORY OF GARDEN STYLES

1. Tom Turner, *Garden History: Philosophy and Design, 2000 BC to 2000 AD* (London: Spon Press, 2005).

SACRED TREES

1. 'Sacred Trees', http://members.tripod.com/holy_98/trees.htm

2. 'Sacred Trees', http://members.tripod.com/holy_98/trees.htm

3. Pradip Krishen, *'Trees of Delhi'*, (India: Dorling Kindersley, 2006).

PHOTO CREDITS